Especially for

....

From

....

Date

....

THE
BIBLE PROMISE
BOOK®

Prayer Edition

BARBOUR
PUBLISHING

© 2013 by Barbour Publishing, Inc.

Prayers are taken from *365 Everyday Prayers* and *365 Everyday Prayers for Men*, published by Barbour Publishing, Inc.

Print ISBN 978-1-62416-641-9

eBook Editions:
Adobe Digital Edition (.epub) 978-1-62836-297-8
Kindle and MobiPocket Edition (.prc) 978-1-62836-298-5

All scripture quotations are taken from the King James Version of the Bible.

Published by Barbour Publishing, Inc., P.O. Box 719, Uhrichsville, Ohio 44683, www.barbourbooks.com

Our mission is to publish and distribute inspirational products offering exceptional value and biblical encouragement to the masses.

 Member of the
Evangelical Christian
Publishers Association

Printed in China.

Contents

INTRODUCTION

❖ ― ・ ― ❖

WHATEVER THE NEED of the moment, the answer can be found in scripture—if we take the time to search for it. Whatever we're feeling, whatever we're suffering, whatever we're hoping, the Bible has something to say to us.

This collection of Bible verses and prayers is meant for use as a handy reference when you need the Bible's guidance on a particular problem in your life or a starting-off point for prayer. It is not meant to replace regular Bible study or the use of a concordance for in-depth study of a subject. There are many facets of your life and many topics in the Bible that are not covered here.

But if, for example, you are struggling with fear or gossip, loneliness or humility, some of the Bible's promises are available to you in these pages. You'll find carefully selected verses for more than five dozen categories, arranged alphabetically for ease of use.

We hope it will be an encouragement to you as you read.

ANGER

———◆—◆—◆———

ANGER IS ONE of those emotions that comes in every shape and size—from quick and reactionary to slow burning, there are few things in this life that can zap our spirit more quickly. When you're tempted to rant and rave, take a deep breath, gather your thoughts, pray, and then—and only then—speak. Leave the rest up to God.

Take this anger from me and make me more like You.
Increase the flow of mercy in my life, Lord.
I want to be just like You. Amen.

The LORD is gracious, and full of compassion;
slow to anger, and of great mercy.
PSALM 145:8

A God ready to pardon, gracious and merciful,
slow to anger, and of great kindness. . .
NEHEMIAH 9:17

For his anger endureth but a moment;
in his favour is life: weeping may endure for
a night but joy cometh in the morning.
PSALM 30:5

Wherefore, my beloved brethren, let every man
be swift to hear, slow to speak, slow to wrath: For the
wrath of man worketh not the righteousness of God.
JAMES 1:19–20

Be not hasty in thy spirit to be angry:
for anger resteth in the bosom of fools.
ECCLESIASTES 7:9

He that is soon angry dealeth foolishly.
PROVERBS 14:17

He that is slow to anger is better than the mighty;
and he that ruleth his spirit than he that taketh a city.
PROVERBS 16:32

In times of violent emotions, Lord, help me to remember
Your unending forgiveness and to treat others
with the kindness and compassion
You show me every day of my life. Amen.

A wrathful man stirreth up strife:
but he that is slow to anger appeaseth strife.
PROVERBS 15:18

An angry man stirreth up strife,
and a furious man aboundeth in transgression.
PROVERBS 29:22

Cease from anger, and forsake wrath:
fret not thyself in any wise to do evil.
PSALM 37:8

Make no friendship with an angry man;
and with a furious man thou shalt not go:
Lest thou learn his ways, and get a snare to thy soul.
PROVERBS 22:24–25

A soft answer turneth away wrath:
but grievous words stir up anger.
PROVERBS 15:1

*Heavenly Father, the next time I am prepared to
lash out at someone who has hurt me, let Your forgiveness
and love be reflected in my response. Amen.*

Fathers, provoke not your children to anger,
lest they be discouraged.
COLOSSIANS 3:21

Be ye angry, and sin not: let not the
sun go down upon your wrath.
EPHESIANS 4:26

The discretion of a man deferreth his anger;
and it is his glory to pass over a transgression.
PROVERBS 19:11

It is better to dwell in the wilderness,
than with a contentious and an angry woman.
PROVERBS 21:19

But I say unto you, That whosoever is
angry with his brother without a cause
shall be in danger of the judgment.
MATTHEW 5:22

*Prosper my relationships, Father, by blessing them with
truthful but gentle words that turn aside anger. Amen.*

Let all bitterness, and wrath, and anger,
and clamour, and evil speaking, be put away from
you, with all malice: And be ye kind one to another,
tenderhearted, forgiving one another, even as
God for Christ's sake hath forgiven you.
EPHESIANS 4:31–32

Wrath is cruel, and anger is outrageous;
but who is able to stand before envy?
PROVERBS 27:4

If thine enemy be hungry, give him bread to eat;
and if he be thirsty, give him water to drink:
For thou shalt heap coals of fire upon his head,
and the LORD shall reward thee.
PROVERBS 25:21–22

Dearly beloved, avenge not yourselves,
but rather give place unto wrath: for it is written,
Vengeance is mine; I will repay, saith the Lord.
Therefore if thine enemy hunger, feed him; if he thirst,
give him drink: for in so doing thou shalt heap
coals of fire on his head. Be not overcome of evil,
but overcome evil with good.

ROMANS 12:19–21

Lord, help me be the peacekeeper,
never the one who stirs up more anger. Amen.

But now ye also put off all these; anger,
wrath, malice, blasphemy, filthy
communication out of your mouth.

COLOSSIANS 3:8

....

....

....

....

....

....

....

....

BELIEF

DO YOU REMEMBER the day that you uttered the words that began your faith walk? Maybe you repeated Peter's great confession: "I believe that Jesus is the Christ—the Son of the living God." What a simple, profound, wonderful truth. No matter what life brings, hold tight to that fundamental belief—and the beliefs you've adopted as you've grown in Christ.

Thank You for making me Your beloved child, Father.
Make me gold; make me strong; help me believe. Amen.

For God so loved the world, that he gave his only
begotten Son, that whosoever believeth in him
should not perish, but have everlasting life.
JOHN 3:16

To him give all the prophets witness,
that through his name whosoever believeth
in him shall receive remission of sins.
ACTS 10:43

As it is written, Behold, I lay in Sion a
stumblingstone and rock of offence: and whosoever
believeth on him shall not be ashamed.
ROMANS 9:33

But as many as received him, to them gave
he power to become the sons of God,
even to them that believe on his name.
JOHN 1:12

He that believeth on him is not condemned:
but he that believeth not is condemned already,
because he hath not believed in the name of
the only begotten Son of God.
JOHN 3:18

He that believeth on the Son hath everlasting life:
and he that believeth not the Son shall not see life;
but the wrath of God abideth on him.

JOHN 3:36

Wherefore also it is contained in the scripture,
Behold, I lay in Sion a chief corner stone, elect,
precious: and he that believeth on him
shall not be confounded.

1 PETER 2:6

*Lord, there is so much I do not understand about You.
Still, I can see the effects of Your actions, the evidence that
You are still active in my daily life. I do not need to physically
see You to believe. Your evidence is everywhere. Amen.*

And they said, Believe on the Lord Jesus Christ,
and thou shalt be saved, and thy house.

ACTS 16:31

I am come a light into the world, that whosoever
believeth on me should not abide in darkness.

JOHN 12:46

And Jesus said unto them, I am the bread of life:
he that cometh to me shall never hunger;
and he that believeth on me shall never thirst.

JOHN 6:35

Jesus said unto him, If thou canst believe,
all things are possible to him that believeth.
MARK 9:23

Jesus saith unto him, Thomas, because thou
hast seen me, thou hast believed: blessed are they
that have not seen, and yet have believed.
JOHN 20:29

*There is no condemnation for us when we believe
in You, Jesus. The covering of Your blood helps us to
prevail over anything. We never need to fear anymore.
Thank You for giving us this victory. Amen.*

Verily, verily, I say unto you, He that
believeth on me hath everlasting life.
JOHN 6:47

CHARITY

THOUGH WE MAY think of charity in financial terms, God doesn't. He calls on us to live generously, sharing not only our finances and goods but our whole lives with others. Whether it is forgiveness or a good meal, we are to withhold nothing from others in need.

Guide me as I choose among many worthy causes;
make me conscious of the blessings You have given me,
Lord. Help me to be a cheerful giver. Amen.

Blessed is he that considereth the poor:
the LORD will deliver him in time of trouble.
The LORD will preserve him, and keep him alive;
and he shall be blessed upon the earth: and thou
wilt not deliver him unto the will of his enemies.

PSALM 41:1–2

He that hath pity upon the poor lendeth
unto the LORD; and that which he hath
given will he pay him again.

PROVERBS 19:17

But when thou makest a feast, call the poor,
the maimed, the lame, the blind: And thou shalt
be blessed; for they cannot recompense thee:
for thou shalt be recompensed at the
resurrection of the just.

LUKE 14:13–14

Sell that ye have, and give alms; provide
yourselves bags which wax not old, a treasure
in the heavens that faileth not, where no thief
approacheth, neither moth corrupteth.

LUKE 12:33

He that despiseth his neighbour sinneth:
but he that hath mercy on the poor, happy is he.

PROVERBS 14:21

Give, and it shall be given unto you;
good measure, pressed down, and shaken together,
and running over, shall men give into your bosom.
For with the same measure that ye mete
withal it shall be measured to you again.
LUKE 6:38

He hath dispersed, he hath given to the poor;
his righteousness endureth for ever;
his horn shall be exalted with honour.
PSALM 112:9

*Remind me, Lord, that though the little I can give seems
useless, when added to the little that millions give, my charity
can make a difference. Help me to give in faith. Amen.*

And now abideth faith, hope, charity,
these three; but the greatest of these is charity.
1 CORINTHIANS 13:13

He that giveth unto the poor shall not lack:
but he that hideth his eyes shall have many a curse.
PROVERBS 28:27

Every man according as he purposeth in his heart,
so let him give; not grudgingly, or of necessity:
for God loveth a cheerful giver.
2 CORINTHIANS 9:7

Then Jesus beholding him loved him,
and said unto him, One thing thou lackest: go thy way,
sell whatsoever thou hast, and give to the poor,
and thou shalt have treasure in heaven: and come,
take up the cross, and follow me.

MARK 10:21

He is ever merciful, and lendeth;
and his seed is blessed.

PSALM 37:26

Lord, prevent me from giving out of a need for
recognition or a desire to be blessed by others.
Let love be at the heart of every gift I give. Amen.

Take heed that ye do not your alms before men,
to be seen of them: otherwise ye have no reward of
your Father which is in heaven. Therefore when thou
doest thine alms, do not sound a trumpet before thee,
as the hypocrites do in the synagogues and in the
streets, that they may have glory of men.
Verily I say unto you, They have their reward.
But when thou doest alms, let not thy left hand
know what thy right hand doeth: That thine alms
may be in secret: and thy Father which seeth
in secret himself shall reward thee openly.

MATTHEW 6:1-4

Then shall the King say unto them on his right hand, Come, ye blessed of my Father, inherit the kingdom prepared for you from the foundation of the world: For I was an hungred, and ye gave me meat: I was thirsty, and ye gave me drink: I was a stranger, and ye took me in: Naked, and ye clothed me: I was sick, and ye visited me: I was in prison, and ye came unto me. Then shall the righteous answer him, saying, Lord, when saw we thee an hungred, and fed thee? or thirsty, and gave thee drink? When saw we thee a stranger, and took thee in? or naked, and clothed thee? Or when saw we thee sick, or in prison, and came unto thee? And the King shall answer and say unto them, Verily I say unto you, Inasmuch as ye have done it unto one of the least of these my brethren, ye have done it unto me.

MATTHEW 25:34-40

CHILDREN

CHILDREN ARE A natural result of the love between a man and his wife, and God has given us a natural instinct to love our own. If we adopt children, the choice is made out of love. Our children will know how much we love them by the way we interact with them. And it's important that they know, because as parents we are a crucial model of their Father in heaven.

Lord, help me to be understanding with my children,
to encourage rather than discourage. I want to
take their hands and walk with them, as You've
taken time to walk with me. Amen.

And they said, Believe on the Lord Jesus Christ,
and thou shalt be saved, and thy house.
ACTS 16:31

For the promise is unto you, and to your children,
and to all that are afar off, even as many as
the LORD our God shall call.
ACTS 2:39

And all thy children shall be taught of the LORD;
and great shall be the peace of thy children.
ISAIAH 54:13

For I will pour water upon him that is thirsty,
and floods upon the dry ground: I will pour my spirit
upon thy seed, and my blessing upon thine offspring.
ISAIAH 44:3

But when Jesus saw it, he was much displeased, and
said unto them, Suffer the little children to come unto
to me, and forbid them not: for of such is the kingdom
of God. Verily I say unto you, Whosoever shall not
receive the kingdom of God as a little child, he shall
not enter therein. And he took them up in his arms,
put his hands upon them, and blessed them.
MARK 10:14–16

Thy wife shall be as a fruitful vine by the sides of thine
house: thy children like olive plants round about thy table.
PSALM 128:3

Lo, children are an heritage of the LORD:
and the fruit of the womb is his reward.
As arrows are in the hand of a mighty man; so are
children of the youth. Happy is the man that hath his
quiver full of them: they shall not be ashamed, but
they shall speak with the enemies in the gate.
PSALM 127:3–5

The rewards of parenting are not always what I expect.
Often they are priceless. Thank You, Father, for these
children and all the blessings they have brought in the past
and will continue to bring in the future. Amen.

Yet setteth he the poor on high from affliction,
and maketh him families like a flock.
PSALM 107:41

Children's children are the crown of old men;
and the glory of children are their fathers.
PROVERBS 17:6

Even a child is known by his doings, whether his work
be pure, and whether it be right.
PROVERBS 20:11

COMFORT

WHERE DO YOU turn for comfort? To a friend or family member? A favorite dessert? The truth is that the only real source of comfort is just a prayer away—God's supply of comfort is always ready and available. All we have to do is ask.

Lord, Your Word says that You are "the God of all comfort."
I desperately need that comfort right now.
Please hold me close and console my heart in a way
that not even my closest friends ever could. Amen.

God is our refuge and strength, a very present
help in trouble. Therefore will not we fear,
though the earth be removed, and though the
mountains be carried into the midst of the sea;
Though the waters thereof roar and be troubled,
though the mountains shake with the swelling thereof.
PSALM 46:1–3

Though I walk in the midst of trouble,
thou wilt revive me: thou shalt stretch forth
thine hand against the wrath of mine enemies,
and thy right hand shall save me.
PSALM 138:7

The LORD is my rock, and my fortress, and my deliverer;
my God, my strength, in whom I will trust; my buckler,
and the horn of my salvation, and my high tower.
PSALM 18:2

For he hath not despised nor abhorred the affliction
of the afflicted; neither hath he hid his face from him;
but when he cried unto him, he heard.
PSALM 22:24

Though he fall, he shall not be utterly cast down:
for the LORD upholdeth him with his hand.
PSALM 37:24

The LORD is good, a strong hold in the day of trouble;
and he knoweth them that trust in him.
NAHUM 1:7

But the salvation of the righteous is of the LORD:
he is their strength in the time of trouble.
PSALM 37:39

Cast thy burden upon the LORD,
and he shall sustain thee: he shall never
suffer the righteous to be moved.
PSALM 55:22

Fill my emptiness with Your unconditional love, Lord.
Make me whole in You as I am comforted
by Your healing Spirit. Amen.

These things I have spoken unto you, that in me
ye might have peace. In the world ye shall have
tribulation: but be of good cheer;
I have overcome the world.
JOHN 16:33

Come unto me, all ye that labour and are heavy laden,
and I will give you rest.
MATTHEW 11:28

For as the sufferings of Christ abound in us,
so our consolation also aboundeth by Christ.
2 CORINTHIANS 1:5

The LORD also will be a refuge for the oppressed,
a refuge in times of trouble.
PSALM 9:9

*Mighty Lord in heaven, grief overwhelms me. I feel alone,
even in the midst of friends and family who have come to
comfort me. Thank You for the comfort only You can give.
Amen.*

For the LORD will not cast off for ever: But though he
cause grief, yet will he have compassion according to
the multitude of his mercies. For he doth not afflict
willingly nor grieve the children of men.
LAMENTATIONS 3:31–33

Wait on the LORD: be of good courage, and he shall
strengthen thine heart: wait, I say, on the LORD.
PSALM 27:14

CONTENTMENT

TOO MANY OF us live in an "if only. . ." state. "If only I
made a larger salary. . ." "If only I found my soulmate. . ."
"If only we would get pregnant. . ." But God calls His
children to live in thankfulness for the blessings we
have now, and the hope of blessings in the future. True
contentment sees Him as the source of every good thing.

*Father, thank You for showing me that contentment
is not a destination but a journey. I pray that I will focus
on what You have given me. May I see my cup as
running over with Your blessings. Amen.*

A merry heart doeth good like a medicine:
but a broken spirit drieth the bones.
PROVERBS 17:22

Let your conversation be without covetousness; and be
content with such things as ye have: for he hath said,
I will never leave thee, nor forsake thee.
HEBREWS 13:5

All the days of the afflicted are evil: but he that is
of a merry heart hath a continual feast.
PROVERBS 15:15

*I know You want the best for me, Lord, and You will provide it.
My job is to live my life in a way that glorifies You. Everything
beyond that is a blessing. I choose to be content. Amen.*

A sound heart is the life of the flesh:
but envy the rottenness of the bones.
PROVERBS 14:30

But godliness with contentment is great gain.
1 TIMOTHY 6:6

Let not thine heart envy sinners: but be thou in the
fear of the LORD all the day long. For surely there is an
end; and thine expectation shall not be cut off.
PROVERBS 23:17–18

CORRECTION, GOD'S

GOD'S CORRECTION ISN'T easy to endure—and we'd rather *not* if we had a choice. But God cares too much about us to leave us the way we are. He wants us to grow spiritually, ever closer to Him.

Father, Your correction lasts only a moment; but its blessings
are eternal. When I realize You are so concerned for me
and want to help me, I am filled with gratitude and
willing to be led in the right direction. Amen.

For whom the LORD loveth he correcteth;
even as a father the son in whom he delighteth.
PROVERBS 3:12

Thou shalt also consider in thine heart, that,
as a man chasteneth his son, so the LORD thy God
chasteneth thee. Therefore thou shalt keep the
commandments of the LORD thy God,
to walk in his ways, and to fear him.
DEUTERONOMY 8:5–6

Blessed is the man whom thou chastenest,
O LORD, and teachest him out of thy law;
That thou mayest give him rest from the days of
adversity, until the pit be digged for the wicked.
PSALM 94:12–13

For which cause we faint not; but though our outward
man perish, yet the inward man is renewed day by day.
For our light affliction, which is but for a moment,
worketh for us a far more exceeding
and eternal weight of glory.
2 CORINTHIANS 4:16–17

But when we are judged, we are chastened of the Lord,
that we should not be condemned with the world.
1 CORINTHIANS 11:32

For they verily for a few days chastened us
after their own pleasure; but he for our profit,
that we might be partakers of his holiness.
Now no chastening for the present seemeth
to be joyous, but grievous: nevertheless afterward
it yieldeth the peaceable fruit of righteousness
unto them which are exercised thereby.
HEBREWS 12:10–11

*Lord, let me know when I am wrong. That way I can come
to You for cleansing and an opportunity to make things right.
Thank You for the truth in Your Word. Amen.*

For whom the Lord loveth he chasteneth,
and scourgeth every son whom he receiveth.
If ye endure chastening, God dealeth with you
as with sons; for what son is he whom
the father chasteneth not?
HEBREWS 12:6–7

COURAGE

WHAT SCENARIOS RUN through your head and leave you shaking in your boots? Confrontations? Public speaking? Talking to others about Jesus? Even if our human nature is to shy away from these situations, the Holy Spirit is the source of courage we need to live boldly for God.

I want to be strong, Lord—in You and for You.
Give me courage each day. When evil seems to abound
and sin distracts me from Your ways, thank You
that Your love abounds still more. Amen.

Wait on the LORD: be of good courage, and he shall
strengthen thine heart: wait, I say, on the LORD.
PSALM 27:14

For the LORD loveth judgment, and forsaketh
not his saints; they are preserved for ever:
but the seed of the wicked shall be cut off.
PSALM 37:28

But now thus saith the LORD that created thee,
O Jacob, and he that formed thee, O Israel,
Fear not: for I have redeemed thee,
I have called thee by thy name; thou art mine.
ISAIAH 43:1

You promise courage and strength when I need them.
In Your power I have done some remarkable things.
Thank You, Lord, for the hidden strength
You give me—Your strength. Amen.

Fear not: for they that be with us are more
than they that be with them.
2 KINGS 6:16

Trust in the LORD, and do good; so shalt thou dwell in
the land, and verily thou shalt be fed.
PSALM 37:3

He giveth power to the faint; and to them that
have no might he increaseth strength.
ISAIAH 40:29

Be of good courage, and he shall strengthen
your heart, all ye that hope in the LORD.
PSALM 31:24

I know both how to be abased, and I know how to
abound: every where and in all things I am instructed
both to be full and to be hungry, both to abound and
to suffer need. I can do all things through
Christ which strengtheneth me.
PHILIPPIANS 4:12–13

DEATH

IN THE BIBLE, death refers both to a physical and spiritual demise, for unrepented sin kills souls as surely as it destroys bodies. But God delivers those who believe in Him from both physical and spiritual destruction.

Father, when my time on earth comes to an end,
I pray I will be able to bear death as well as I bore life,
secure in Your love and looking to the salvation
You have promised is mine. Amen.

Yea, though I walk through the valley of the shadow
of death, I will fear no evil: for thou art with me;
thy rod and thy staff they comfort me.
PSALM 23:4

O death, where is thy sting?
O grave, where is thy victory?
1 CORINTHIANS 15:55

The wicked is driven away in his wickedness:
but the righteous hath hope in his death.
PROVERBS 14:32

*I know that death comes to us all, Lord, but sometimes
I feel I cannot give up a loved one. In a time such as this,
send me Your comfort and peace, I pray. Amen.*

Much more then, being now justified by his blood,
we shall be saved from wrath through him.
ROMANS 5:9

Forasmuch then as the children are partakers
of flesh and blood, he also himself likewise took
part of the same; that through death he might destroy
him that had the power of death, that is, the devil;
And deliver them who through fear of death
were all their lifetime subject to bondage.
HEBREWS 2:14–15

Verily, verily, I say unto you, If a man keep my saying,
he shall never see death.
JOHN 8:51

For this God is our God for ever and ever:
he will be our guide even unto death.
PSALM 48:14

But God will redeem my soul from the power
of the grave: for he shall receive me.
PSALM 49:15

Be with me today, Father, as I grieve.
Wipe away my tears and give me faith in these dark hours,
for You have already triumphed over death. Amen.

My flesh and my heart faileth: but God is the
strength of my heart, and my portion for ever.
PSALM 73:26

He will swallow up death in victory;
and the Lord GOD will wipe away
tears from off all faces.
ISAIAH 25:8

I will ransom them from the power of the grave;
I will redeem them from death: O death, I will be
thy plagues; O grave, I will be thy destruction:
repentance shall be hid from mine eyes.

Hosea 13:14

Precious in the sight of the Lord
is the death of his saints.

Psalm 116:15

Mark the perfect man, and behold the upright:
for the end of that man is peace.

Psalm 37:37

But though our outward man perish,
yet the inward man is renewed day by day.

2 Corinthians 4:16

For I am persuaded, that neither death, nor life,
nor angels, nor principalities, nor powers,
nor things present, nor things to come,
Nor height, nor depth, nor any other creature,
shall be able to separate us from the love of God,
which is in Christ Jesus our Lord.

Romans 8:38–39

ENEMIES

IT'S EASY TO be discouraged when it feels like the entire world is against you. The truth is, God cares about those frustrations you feel—and He promises over and over in His Word that He will fight for us to make His will prevail.

You have promised the righteous Your protection from their enemies, Lord. Such protection is beyond my understanding. Thank You for Your help when I call on You. Amen.

And the LORD shall help them, and deliver them:
he shall deliver them from the wicked,
and save them, because they trust in him.
PSALM 37:40

For the rod of the wicked shall not rest upon
the lot of the righteous; lest the righteous
put forth their hands unto iniquity.
PSALM 125:3

*As I firmly stand on Your Word and do what is right,
Lord, I ask You to bring victory as You have promised.
Help me show Your love to those who gather against me.
Open their eyes to know You. Amen.*

His heart is established, he shall not be afraid,
until he see his desire upon his enemies.
PSALM 112:8

Thy right hand, O LORD, is become glorious in power:
thy right hand, O LORD, hath dashed
in pieces the enemy.
EXODUS 15:6

Be not afraid of sudden fear, neither of
the desolation of the wicked, when it cometh.
For the LORD shall be thy confidence,
and shall keep thy foot from being taken.
PROVERBS 3:25-26

Through God we shall do valiantly:
for he it is that shall tread down our enemies.
PSALM 60:12

No weapon that is formed against thee shall prosper;
and every tongue that shall rise against
thee in judgment thou shalt condemn.
This is the heritage of the servants of the LORD,
and their righteousness is of me, saith the LORD.
ISAIAH 54:17

When a man's ways please the LORD,
he maketh even his enemies to be at peace with him.
PROVERBS 16:7

The LORD taketh my part with them that help me:
therefore shall I see my desire upon them that hate me.
PSALM 118:7

That he would grant unto us, that we being
delivered out of the hand of our enemies
might serve him without fear.

LUKE 1:74

The LORD shall cause thine enemies that rise up against
thee to be smitten before thy face: they shall come out
against thee one way, and flee before thee seven ways.

DEUTERONOMY 28:7

*Father, it often seems that might makes right and
I stand no chance, but I know Your power can overcome
whatever evil men might plan. When I am in despair,
fill me with faith in Your justice. Amen.*

For the LORD your God is he that goeth with you,
to fight for you against your enemies, to save you.

DEUTERONOMY 20:4

And shall not God avenge his own elect, which cry day
and night unto him, though he bear long with them?

LUKE 18:7

Behold, they shall surely gather together,
but not by me: whosoever shall gather together
against thee shall fall for thy sake.

ISAIAH 54:15

That we should be saved from our enemies,
and from the hand of all that hate us.
LUKE 1:71

Ye that love the LORD, hate evil: he preserveth
the souls of his saints; he delivereth them
out of the hand of the wicked.
PSALM 97:10

If I obey You, Father God, I will have nothing to fear from
my critics. Fill my ears with Your words so I won't hear
the complaints of those who hate You. Amen.

But I will deliver thee in that day, saith the LORD:
and thou shalt not be given into the hand of the men
of whom thou art afraid. For I will surely deliver thee,
and thou shalt not fall by the sword, but thy life shall
be for a prey unto thee: because thou hast put
thy trust in me, saith the LORD.
JEREMIAH 39:17–18

But the LORD your God ye shall fear; and he shall
deliver you out of the hand of all your enemies.
2 KINGS 17:39

And he answered, Fear not: for they that be
with us are more than they that be with them.
2 KINGS 6:16

So that we may boldly say, The Lord is my helper,
and I will not fear what man shall do unto me.
HEBREWS 13:6

ETERNAL LIFE

THOUGH GOD DOES not tell us every detail about eternity, He provides us the road map to get there. Eternal life is available only to those who trust in His Son. Though we have earned death through sin, in Jesus we are brought to a new, eternal life.

Forever, Lord, what encouragement is in that word. We have all eternity to spend with You in heaven. Thank You for this indescribable gift. Thank You for being the Alpha and the Omega, the first and the last. Amen.

Verily, verily I say unto you, He that believeth
on me hath everlasting life.
JOHN 6:47

Jesus said unto her, I am the resurrection, and the life:
he that believeth in me, though he were dead,
yet shall he live: And whosoever liveth and believeth
in me shall never die. Believest thou this?
JOHN 11:25–26

Behold, I shew you a mystery; We shall not all sleep,
but we shall all be changed, In a moment, in the
twinkling of an eye, at the last trump: for the trumpet
shall sound, and the dead shall be raised incorruptible,
and we shall be changed. For this corruptible must
put on incorruption, and this mortal must put on
immortality. So when this corruptible shall have put
on incorruption, and this mortal shall have put on
immortality, then shall be brought to pass the saying
that is written, Death is swallowed up in victory.
1 CORINTHIANS 15:51–54

And this is the promise that he hath
promised us, even eternal life.
1 JOHN 2:25

For the Lord himself shall descend from heaven with a shout, with the voice of the archangel, and with the trump of God: and the dead in Christ shall rise first.
1 THESSALONIANS 4:16

For since by man came death, by man came also the resurrection of the dead.
1 CORINTHIANS 15:21

You, Lord Jesus, are always my goal. You are the end of my path; my eternal reward is to live with You forever. Thank You that my way leads to Your eternal home. Amen.

These things have I written unto you that believe on the name of the Son of God; that ye may know that ye have eternal life, and that ye may believe on the name of the Son of God.
1 JOHN 5:13

Marvel not at this: for the hour is coming, in the which all that are in the graves shall hear his voice, And shall come forth; they that have done good, unto the resurrection of life; and they that have done evil, unto the resurrection of damnation.
JOHN 5:28-29

For he that soweth to his flesh shall of the flesh reap
corruption; but he that soweth to the Spirit
shall of the Spirit reap life everlasting.
GALATIANS 6:8

For we know that if our earthly house of this
tabernacle were dissolved, we have a building of God,
an house not made with hands, eternal in the heavens.
2 CORINTHIANS 5:1

*Father, I look forward to wearing the crown of eternal life.
I know I can never earn that priceless gift. You freely give
it to me and all who will accept it. Thank You. Amen.*

And many of them that sleep in the dust of the earth
shall awake, some to everlasting life, and some to
shame and everlasting contempt.
DANIEL 12:2

Thy dead men shall live, together with my dead body
shall they arise. Awake and sing, ye that dwell in dust:
for thy dew is as the dew of herbs,
and the earth shall cast out the dead.
ISAIAH 26:19

For God so loved the world, that he gave his only
begotten Son, that whosoever believeth in him
should not perish, but have everlasting life.
JOHN 3:16

For thou wilt not leave my soul in hell; neither wilt
thou suffer thine Holy One to see corruption.
PSALM 16:10

But is now made manifest by the appearing of our
Saviour Jesus Christ, who hath abolished death,
and hath brought life and immortality
to light through the gospel.
2 TIMOTHY 1:10

*Help me see the value of patiently enduring hardship.
I look forward with joy to eternity with You. Strengthen me,
Lord, to be patient until that day. Amen.*

And this is the record, that God hath given
to us eternal life, and this life is in his Son.
1 JOHN 5:11

In my Father's house are many mansions: if it were
not so, I would have told you. I go to prepare a place
for you. And if I go and prepare a place for you,
I will come again, and receive you unto myself;
that where I am, there ye may be also.
JOHN 14:2-3

FAITH

FAITH IS AN amazing interaction between God and humans. Our Lord calls us to trust, and through the salvation He offers in Jesus, we believe and begin a life-journey of faith.

Lord God, my faith in You is not based in my senses or my intellect but in Your never-failing love, which saved my soul and promises me unspeakable joy. Amen.

Now faith is the substance of things hoped for,
the evidence of things not seen.
HEBREWS 11:1

Watch ye, stand fast in the faith,
quit you like men, be strong.
1 CORINTHIANS 16:13

If any of you lack wisdom, let him ask of God,
that giveth to all men liberally, and upbraideth not;
and it shall be given him. But let him ask in faith,
nothing wavering. For he that wavereth is like a
wave of the sea driven with the wind and tossed.
JAMES 1:5–6

As ye have therefore received Christ Jesus the Lord,
so walk ye in him: Rooted and built up in him,
and stablished in the faith, as ye have been taught,
abounding therein with thanksgiving.
COLOSSIANS 2:6–7

For by grace are ye saved through faith;
and that not of yourselves: it is the gift of God.
EPHESIANS 2:8

For ye are all the children of God
by faith in Christ Jesus.
GALATIANS 3:26

The fruit of the Spirit is love, joy, peace, longsuffering,
gentleness, goodness, faith, Meekness,
temperance: against such there is no law.
GALATIANS 5:22–23

*Lord, my faith seems weak—not the type of faith that
might bring victory. But in You I have assurance of victory.
I've read the story, and in the end You will reign victorious.
I praise You, Lord. Amen.*

But continue thou in the things which thou hast
learned and hast been assured of, knowing of whom
thou hast learned them; And that from a child
thou hast known the holy scriptures, which
are able to make thee wise unto salvation
through faith which is in Christ Jesus.
2 TIMOTHY 3:14–15

For we walk by faith, not by sight.
2 CORINTHIANS 5:7

And Jesus answering saith unto them, Have faith in
God. For verily I say unto you, That whosoever shall
say unto this mountain, Be thou removed, and be thou
cast into the sea; and shall not doubt in his heart,
but shall believe that those things which he saith
shall come to pass; he shall have whatsoever he saith.
MARK 11:22–23

*Lord, help me realize that my understanding is not necessary
for the completion of Your plan. You understand everything;
all I need to do is have faith. Amen.*

That Christ may dwell in your hearts by faith; that ye,
being rooted and grounded in love, May be able to
comprehend with all saints what is the breadth,
and length, and depth, and height; And to know
the love of Christ, which passeth knowledge,
that ye might be filled with all the fulness of God.
EPHESIANS 3:17–19

I am crucified with Christ: nevertheless I live; yet not I,
but Christ liveth in me: and the life which I now live in
the flesh I live by the faith of the Son of God,
who loved me, and gave himself for me.
GALATIANS 2:20

He that cometh to God must believe that he is,
and that he is a rewarder of them that
diligently seek him.
HEBREWS 11:6

Wherefore seeing we also are compassed about with
so great a cloud of witnesses, let us lay aside every
weight, and the sin which doth so easily beset us, and
let us run with patience the race that is set before us,
Looking unto Jesus the author and finisher of our
faith; who for the joy that was set before him endured
the cross, despising the shame, and is set down
at the right hand of the throne of God.
HEBREWS 12:1–2

FAITHFULNESS, GOD'S

HAVE YOU EVER broken a promise? Or has someone ever broken a promise to you? It hurts, doesn't it? But God, by His very nature, is forever faithful. In His Word, He tells us He will keep that word. You can count on it!

Lord, like Your long-ago followers, I want to cling to You. Let me not waver in my faith as I follow You. May my life become a testimony to Your faithfulness. Amen.

Know therefore that the LORD thy God, he is
God, the faithful God, which keepeth covenant
and mercy with them that love him and keep
his commandments to a thousand generations.
DEUTERONOMY 7:9

(For the LORD thy God is a merciful God;) he will
not forsake thee, neither destroy thee, nor forget the
covenant of thy fathers which he sware unto them.
DEUTERONOMY 4:31

*I praise You, Lord, for the faithfulness that is part of Your
perfect nature. It never changes or leaves me helpless.
May it seep into my heart and soul as I follow You. Amen.*

He hath remembered his covenant for ever, the word
which he commanded to a thousand generations.
PSALM 105:8

God is not a man, that he should lie;
neither the son of man, that he should repent:
hath he said, and shall he not do it? or hath he spoken,
and shall he not make it good?
NUMBERS 23:19

Let us hold fast the profession of our faith without wavering; (for he is faithful that promised).
HEBREWS 10:23

If we believe not, yet he abideth faithful: he cannot deny himself.
2 TIMOTHY 2:13

The Lord is not slack concerning his promise, as some men count slackness; but is longsuffering to us-ward.
2 PETER 3:9

Blessed be the LORD, that hath given rest unto his people Israel, according to all that he promised: there hath not failed one word of all his good promise.
1 KINGS 8:56

O Lord, thou art my God; I will exalt thee, I will praise thy name; for thou hast done wonderful things; thy counsels of old are faithfulness and truth.
ISAIAH 25:1

And they that know thy name will put their trust in thee: for thou, LORD, hast not forsaken them that seek thee.
PSALM 9:10

Thy word is true from the beginning: and every one
of thy righteous judgments endureth for ever.
PSALM 119:160

For ever, O LORD, thy word is settled in heaven.
Thy faithfulness is unto all generations.
PSALM 119:89–90

*There are times, Lord, when I feel as if You've forgotten me.
How could I let those feelings of being forsaken overwhelm
me? Help me to remember that the Creator of the entire
universe holds me in His hands! Amen.*

And also the Strength of Israel will not lie nor repent:
for he is not a man, that he should repent.
1 SAMUEL 15:29

For all the promises of God in him are yea,
and in him Amen, unto the glory of God by us.
2 CORINTHIANS 1:20

My covenant will I not break, nor alter
the thing that is gone out of my lips.
PSALM 89:34

FEAR

THERE ARE TWO kinds of fear: fear of (or reverence for) God and the doubtful fear that focuses on the things that might go wrong in our lives. Fear of God is a good thing, because it draws us closer to Him in respect and love. But doubtful fears show our lack of reliance on Him.

In the dark of the night I sometimes find myself in the clutch of fear. Because I am Your adopted child through Christ, I know You love me, and I cry out to You. Thank You, Father, for calming and protecting me as I pray. Amen.

And he said unto them,
Why are ye so fearful? how is it that ye have no faith?
MARK 4:40

Fear not, little flock; for it is your Father's good
pleasure to give you the kingdom.
LUKE 12:32

For I the LORD thy God will hold thy right hand,
saying unto thee, Fear not; I will help thee.
ISAIAH 41:13

Your promise tells me I have nothing to fear.
What can I lose that is not already in Your hand?
Thank You for Your protection. Keep me from fear
and strengthen my trust in You. Amen.

But whoso hearkeneth unto me shall dwell safely,
and shall be quiet from fear of evil.
PROVERBS 1:33

And fear not them which kill the body,
but are not able to kill the soul.
MATTHEW 10:28

Be not afraid of sudden fear, neither of
the desolation of the wicked, when it cometh.
For the LORD shall be thy confidence,
and shall keep thy foot from being taken.
PROVERBS 3:25–26

For God hath not given us the spirit of fear;
but of power, and of love, and of a sound mind.
2 TIMOTHY 1:7

The LORD shall give thee rest from thy sorrow,
and from thy fear, and from the hard bondage
wherein thou wast made to serve.
ISAIAH 14:3

When thou liest down, thou shalt not be afraid: yea,
thou shalt lie down, and thy sleep shall be sweet.
PROVERBS 3:24

For the eyes of the Lord are over the righteous,
and his ears are open unto their prayers:
but the face of the Lord is against them that do evil.
And who is he that will harm you, if ye be followers
of that which is good? But and if ye suffer for
righteousness' sake, happy are ye: and be not afraid
of their terror, neither be troubled.
1 PETER 3:12–14

In righteousness shalt thou be established: thou shalt be far from oppression; for thou shalt not fear: and from terror; for it shall not come near thee.

ISAIAH 54:14

For ye have not received the spirit of bondage again to fear; but ye have received the Spirit of adoption, whereby we cry, Abba, Father.

ROMANS 8:15

Heavenly Father, calm my quaking heart. I'd rather turn and run from the circumstances ahead than face them. Give me the strength to move forward, to face my fears with the supernatural courage that comes from Your throne. Amen.

So that we may boldly say, The Lord is my helper, and I will not fear what man shall do unto me.

HEBREWS 13:6

God is our refuge and strength, a very present help in trouble.

PSALM 46:1

The fear of man bringeth a snare: but whoso putteth his trust in the LORD shall be safe.

PROVERBS 29:25

I, even I, am he that comforteth you: who art thou,
that thou shouldest be afraid of a man that shall die,
and of the son of man which shall be made as grass.
ISAIAH 51:12

He shall cover thee with his feathers, and under his
wings shalt thou trust: his truth shall be thy shield
and buckler. Thou shalt not be afraid for the terror
by night; nor for the arrow that flieth by day;
Nor for the pestilence that walketh in darkness;
nor for the destruction that wasteth at noonday.
PSALM 91:4–6

*Father, give me the courage I need to control my fears.
I know that You love me and watch over those I love far
better than I can. Strengthen my heart. Amen.*

Fear not; for thou shalt not be ashamed:
neither be thou confounded.
ISAIAH 54:4

When thou passest through the waters,
I will be with thee; and through the rivers,
they shall not overflow thee: when thou walkest
through the fire, thou shalt not be burned;
neither shall the flame kindle upon thee.
ISAIAH 43:2

Yea, though I walk through the valley of the shadow of
death, I will fear no evil: for thou art with me;
thy rod and thy staff they comfort me. Thou preparest
a table before me in the presence of mine enemies:
thou anointest my head with oil; my cup runneth over.
PSALM 23:4–5

FOOD AND CLOTHING

THOUGH WEALTH AND possessions are gifts from God, they can also distract believers from the fact that this life is temporary. However many things God gives us and the many needs He meets, He asks us to share generously. That's how we store up treasures in heaven.

Thank You for Your care for each of Your children, Lord. I will turn my heart to You for provision for my body and soul. Amen.

And ye shall eat in plenty, and be satisfied,
and praise the name of the LORD your God,
that hath dealt wondrously with you:
and my people shall never be ashamed.

JOEL 2:26

He maketh peace in thy borders,
and filleth thee with the finest of the wheat.

PSALM 147:14

He hath given meat unto them that fear him:
he will ever be mindful of his covenant.

PSALM 111:5

*Father, I am quick to focus on those things that affect me
most directly. Often, I confess, I improperly view my wants as
essentials. Help me keep my attitude in check. Amen.*

The righteous eateth to the satisfying of his soul:
but the belly of the wicked shall want.

PROVERBS 13:25

I will abundantly bless her provision:
I will satisfy her poor with bread.

PSALM 132:15

Therefore take no thought, saying, What shall we eat? or, What shall we drink? or, Wherewithal shall we be clothed? (For after all these things do the Gentiles seek:) for your heavenly Father knoweth that ye have need of all these things.

MATTHEW 6:31–32

FORGIVENESS

FORGIVENESS IS A huge part of the Christian life. God has forgiven us for our sins, and we in turn are to forgive others. Sound tough? It is—unless we have the help of His Spirit.

Father, thanks to You I get to start over, fresh and clean, because You have made me a new person. I now have a lifetime of new days to spend following You. Thank You for Your never-ending forgiveness. Amen.

But I say unto you, Love your enemies, bless them
that curse you, do good to them that hate you,
and pray for them which despitefully use you,
and persecute you; That ye may be the children
of your Father which is in heaven: for he maketh
his sun to rise on the evil and on the good, and
sendeth rain on the just and on the unjust.
Matthew 5:44-45

And when ye stand praying, forgive, if ye have
ought against any: that your Father also which
is in heaven may forgive you your trespasses.
But if ye do not forgive, neither will your Father
which is in heaven forgive your trespasses.
Mark 11:25-26

For if ye forgive men their trespasses,
your heavenly Father will also forgive you.
Matthew 6:14

Therefore if thine enemy hunger, feed him;
if he thirst, give him drink.
Romans 12:20

But love ye your enemies, and do good, and lend,
hoping for nothing again; and your reward shall be
great, and ye shall be the children of the Highest:
for he is kind unto the unthankful and to the evil.
Be ye therefore merciful, as your Father also is
merciful. Judge not, and ye shall not be judged:
condemn not, and ye shall not be condemned:
forgive, and ye shall be forgiven.

LUKE 6:35–37

FRUITFULNESS

WHETHER WE ALWAYS think about it, we are spiritual fruit producers. As we live day by day, others should see the love, faith, and goodness that flow from our lives as we serve Jesus. As we grow in Him, our lives testify to His greatness and the work He's doing in us.

My soul flourishes, Lord, like a well-watered garden carefully tended by Your hand. Thank You for nourishing my life and making it fruitful. Amen.

I am the true vine, and my Father is the husbandman.
Every branch in me that beareth not fruit he taketh
away: and every branch that beareth fruit, he purgeth
it, that it may bring forth more fruit. Now ye are
clean through the word which I have spoken unto you.
Abide in me, and I in you. As the branch cannot bear
fruit of itself, except it abide in the vine; no more can
ye, except ye abide in me. I am the vine, ye are the
branches: He that abideth in me, and I in him,
the same bringeth forth much fruit:
for without me ye can do nothing.

JOHN 15:1–5

And he shall be like a tree planted by the rivers of
water, that bringeth forth his fruit in his season;
his leaf also shall not wither; and whatsoever
he doeth shall prosper.

PSALM 1:3

Therefore they shall come and sing in the height of
Zion, and shall flow together to the goodness
of the LORD, for wheat, and for wine, and for oil,
and for the young of the flock and of the herd:
and their soul shall be as a watered garden;
and they shall not sorrow any more at all.

JEREMIAH 31:12

They shall still bring forth fruit in old age;
they shall be fat and flourishing.
PSALM 92:14

I will be as the dew unto Israel: he shall grow
as the lily, and cast forth his roots as Lebanon.
HOSEA 14:5

*Thank You, Lord, for Your promise that if I am true to You,
You will take care of me and I will produce good fruit.
What I cannot do on my own, You will accomplish,
if I trust in You. Amen.*

For if these things be in you, and abound, they make
you that ye shall neither be barren nor unfruitful in
the knowledge of our Lord Jesus Christ.
2 PETER 1:8

GOSSIP

THERE ARE FEW things in this life more damaging than gossip. Our moms were right when they told us, "If you don't have something nice to say, don't say anything at all." Before talking about someone else, take a moment and think: Am I helping or hurting this situation?

Lord, I pray that I will put my mind in gear before putting my mouth in motion. Instead of causing division and hurt, let my words uplift and bless. I pray that my conversations will bring unity and hope. Amen.

Thou shalt not go up and down as a talebearer
among thy people: neither shalt thou stand against
the blood of thy neighbour; I am the LORD.
LEVITICUS 19:16

The words of a talebearer are as wounds, and
they go down into the innermost parts of the belly.
PROVERBS 18:8

He that goeth about as a talebearer revealeth secrets:
therefore meddle not with him that
flattereth with his lips.
PROVERBS 20:19

*Dear Father, may my words today show that
I recognize You as the source of all good things.
I appreciate Your mercy toward me. Amen.*

A talebearer revealeth secrets: but he that is
of a faithful spirit concealeth the matter.
PROVERBS 11:13

A froward man soweth strife:
and a whisperer separateth chief friends.
PROVERBS 16:28

The tongue deviseth mischiefs;
like a sharp razor, working deceitfully.
PSALM 52:2

Where no wood is, there the fire goeth out:
so where there is no talebearer, the strife ceaseth.
As coals are to burning coals, and wood to fire;
so is a contentious man to kindle strife.
The words of a talebearer are as wounds,
and they go down into the
innermost parts of the belly.
PROVERBS 26:20–22

The north wind driveth away rain:
so doth an angry countenance
a backbiting tongue.
PROVERBS 25:23

Keep thy tongue from evil,
and thy lips from speaking guile.
PSALM 34:13

....
....
....
....
....

GRACE, GROWTH IN

GOD HAS GIVEN us His unmerited favor—His grace. When we couldn't save ourselves, He made a way for us, through His Son. As we recognize our need for grace and appreciate its work in our lives, God pours out His blessings in and through us.

Thank You, Father, for Your generous grace.
I ask that it flow over me again, and always. Amen.

We are bound to thank God always for you, brethren,
as it is meet, because that your faith groweth
exceedingly, and the charity of every one of you
all toward each other aboundeth.

Thank You, Lord, for providing so much growth potential in
Your Word. Make Your truths real to me, Lord. I want to
grow in You and reach out to a world in pain. Amen.

And beside this, giving all diligence, add to
your faith virtue; and to virtue knowledge.

The righteous also shall hold on his way, and he that
hath clean hands shall be stronger and stronger.

GUILT

ONCE WE RECEIVE forgiveness for sin, God doesn't remember our failures—so why do we insist on letting them creep back into our thoughts? We are free in Christ! Free from our past, free from our sin, and free from our guilt!

Faithful Lord, Your love and mercy are wells that never run dry. Thank You for casting my sins away without keeping a record of my failures. Amen.

If we confess our sins, he is faithful and just to forgive
us our sins, and to cleanse us from all unrighteousness.
1 JOHN 1:9

Let the wicked forsake his way, and the unrighteous
man his thoughts: and let him return unto the LORD,
and he will have mercy upon him; and to our God,
for he will abundantly pardon.
ISAIAH 55:7

For the LORD your God is gracious and merciful,
and will not turn away his face from you,
if ye return unto him.
2 CHRONICLES 30:9

*You know my heart, Lord. You know how much
I long to be the person You created me to be.
Please make me new again. Give me a fresh start.
Cover me once again with Your forgiveness. Amen.*

As far as the east is from the west, so far hath
he removed our transgressions from us.
PSALM 103:12

For if our heart condemn us, God is greater
than our heart, and knoweth all things.
1 JOHN 3:20

For I will be merciful to their unrighteousness, and
their sins and their iniquities will I remember no more.
HEBREWS 8:12

Therefore if any man be in Christ, he is a new creature:
old things are passed away;
behold, all things are become new.
2 CORINTHIANS 5:17

For I will forgive their iniquity,
and I will remember their sin no more.
JEREMIAH 31:34

*I confess I haven't followed Your will for my life. Please
forgive me, Lord, and make my life new. Turn my heart from
its self-centered path to one that is focused on You. Amen.*

And I will cleanse them from all their iniquity,
whereby they have sinned against me; and I will
pardon all their iniquities, whereby they have sinned,
and whereby they have transgressed against me.
JEREMIAH 33:8

I write unto you, little children, because your sins
are forgiven you for his name's sake.
1 JOHN 2:12

I, even I, am he that blotteth out thy transgressions
for mine own sake, and will not remember thy sins.
ISAIAH 43:25

But if we walk in the light, as he is in the light, we have
fellowship one with another, and the blood of Jesus
Christ his Son cleanseth us from all sin.
1 JOHN 1:7

HELP IN TROUBLES

TROUBLES COME. IT'S a fact of life, even (or especially) for Christians. But the God who has overcome the world also overcomes our day-to-day difficulties. Nothing is too big (or too small) for Him!

I know that as a Christian I need not fear the storms of life.
When I feel afraid, help me to focus my eyes on You, Lord.
Amen.

But the salvation of the righteous is of the LORD:
he is their strength in the time of trouble.
PSALM 37:39

The LORD openeth the eyes of the blind:
the LORD raiseth them that are bowed down:
the LORD loveth the righteous.
PSALM 146:8

The LORD is good, a strong hold in the day of trouble;
and he knoweth them that trust in him.
NAHUM 1:7

*You never promised my life would be easy,
Lord, but You do promise to be there for me in good times
and bad, supporting me and leading me back into the light.
You are my strength and power. Amen.*

Though he fall, he shall not be utterly cast down:
for the LORD upholdeth him with his hand.
PSALM 37:24

Thou art my hiding place; thou shalt preserve me
from trouble; thou shalt compass me about
with songs of deliverance.
PSALM 32:7

Thou, which hast shewed me great and sore troubles,
shalt quicken me again, and shalt bring me up
again from the depths of the earth.
PSALM 71:20

Why art thou cast down, O my soul? and why art
thou disquieted within me? hope thou in God:
for I shall yet praise him, who is the health
of my countenance, and my God.
PSALM 42:11

My flesh and my heart faileth: but God is the
strength of my heart, and my portion for ever.
PSALM 73:26

There shall no evil befall thee, neither shall any plague
come nigh thy dwelling. For he shall give his angels
charge over thee, to keep thee in all thy ways.
PSALM 91:10–11

They that sow in tears shall reap in joy.
He that goeth forth and weepeth, bearing precious
seed, shall doubtless come again with rejoicing,
bringing his sheaves with him.
PSALM 126:5–6

O love the LORD, all ye his saints: for the LORD
preserveth the faithful, and plentifully
rewardeth the proud doer.

PSALM 31:23

Though ye have lien among the pots,
yet shall ye be as the wings of a dove covered
with silver, and her feathers with yellow gold.

PSALM 68:13

*You give me strength to continue when troubles assail me,
by filling my heart with hope. As I trust in You,
Lord, strength fills my entire being.
Whether I face hard times or good ones,
You are forever the focus of my heart. Amen.*

The LORD is my strength and my shield; my heart
trusted in him, and I am helped: therefore my heart
greatly rejoiceth; and with my song will I praise him.

PSALM 28:7

The LORD also will be a refuge for the oppressed,
a refuge in times of trouble.

PSALM 9:9

For he hath not despised nor abhorred the affliction
of the afflicted; neither hath he hid his face from him;
but when he cried unto him, he heard.
PSALM 22:24

Though I walk in the midst of trouble,
thou wilt revive me: thou shalt stretch forth
thine hand against the wrath of mine enemies,
and thy right hand shall save me.
PSALM 138:7

*Father, give me Your peace and an understanding that all
things work together for good when I follow Your will. Amen.*

Many are the afflictions of the righteous:
but the LORD delivereth him out of them all.
PSALM 34:19

For the LORD will not cast off for ever:
But though he cause grief, yet will he have compassion
according to the multitude of his mercies. For he doth
not afflict willingly nor grieve the children of men.
LAMENTATIONS 3:31–33

The LORD is my rock, and my fortress, and my deliverer;
my God, my strength, in whom I will trust; my buckler,
and the horn of my salvation, and my high tower.
PSALM 18:2

These things I have spoken unto you, that in me
ye might have peace. In the world ye shall have
tribulation: but be of good cheer;
I have overcome the world.
JOHN 16:33

HOLY SPIRIT

THE HOLY SPIRIT indwells Christians, making us able to live for God in a sin-filled world. Through the Spirit, God sends us on a heavenly mission: to share His good news with the world around us. Only by living in the Spirit can we have success in this job.

Wherever I go, I cannot separate myself from Your Spirit, Lord. Draw me near to You through Your Spirit's power. Amen.

Behold, I will pour out my spirit unto you,
I will make known my words unto you.
PROVERBS 1:23

And I will pray the Father, and he shall give you
another Comforter, that he may abide with you for
ever; Even the Spirit of truth; whom the world cannot
receive, because it seeth him not, neither knoweth him:
but ye know him; for he dwelleth with you,
and shall be in you.
JOHN 14:16–17

He that believeth on me, as the scripture hath said,
out of his belly shall flow rivers of living water.
(But this spake he of the Spirit, which they that believe
on him should receive: for the Holy Ghost was not yet
given; because that Jesus was not yet glorified.)
JOHN 7:38–39

Howbeit when he, the Spirit of truth, is come,
he will guide you into all truth: for he shall not speak
of himself; but whatsoever he shall hear, that shall he
speak: and he will shew you things to come.
JOHN 16:13

As for me, this is my convenant with them, saith the
LORD; My spirit that is upon thee, and my words which
I have put in thy mouth, shall not depart out of thy
mouth, nor out of the mouth of thy seed, nor out of
the mouth of thy seed's seed, saith the LORD,
from henceforth and for ever.

ISAIAH 59:21

Turn my spirit toward You again, Lord,
where I can find the joy and contentment I'm missing.
May I feel Your Spirit touch my heart, so that I may
bring good to those I see each day. Amen.

If ye then, being evil, know how to give good gifts unto
your children: how much more shall your heavenly
Father give the Holy Spirit to them that ask him?

LUKE 11:13

But whosoever drinketh of the water that
I shall give him shall never thirst; but the water that
I shall give him shall be in him a well of water
springing up into everlasting life.

JOHN 4:14

And I will put my spirit within you,
and cause you to walk in my statutes,
and ye shall keep my judgments, and do them.
EZEKIEL 36:27

That the blessing of Abraham might come on the
Gentiles through Jesus Christ; that we might receive
the promise of the Spirit through faith.
GALATIANS 3:14

In my own power, Lord, I know I'm too weak.
But I have faith You will enable me to meet
whatever challenges life brings. I'll wait for You,
Lord, to empower me with Your Spirit. Amen.

But the anointing which ye have received of him
abideth in you, and ye need not that any man teach
you: but as the same anointing teacheth you of all
things, and is truth, and is no lie, and even as
it hath taught you, ye shall abide in him.
1 JOHN 2:27

For the kingdom of God is not meat and drink; but
righteousness, and peace, and joy in the Holy Ghost.
ROMANS 14:17

Likewise the Spirit also helpeth our infirmities:
for we know not what we should pray for as we ought:
but the Spirit itself maketh intercession for us with
groanings which cannot be uttered. And he that
searcheth the hearts knoweth what is the mind
of the Spirit, because he maketh intercession
for the saints according to the will of God.

ROMANS 8:26–27

For ye have not received the spirit of bondage again
to fear; but ye have received the Spirit of adoption,
whereby we cry, Abba, Father.

ROMANS 8:15

HONESTY

FEW OF US would consider ourselves "liars." But most of us *are* guilty now and then of "little, white lies." Maybe we want to avoid confrontation or to smooth over an issue with friends or family. In God's eyes, though, honesty is a black-and-white issue. Commit always to speaking the truth. . .in love.

Lord, guide me daily to commit to being truthful.
Help me as I strive to be like You. Amen.

Ye shall not steal, neither deal falsely,
neither lie one to another.
LEVITICUS 19:11

Are there yet the treasures of wickedness in the
house of the wicked, and the scant measure that is
abominable? Shall I count them pure with the wicked
balances, and with the bag of deceitful weights?
For the rich men thereof are full of violence,
and the inhabitants thereof have spoken lies,
and their tongue is deceitful in their mouth.
MICAH 6:10–12

Ye shall do no unrighteousness in judgment,
in meteyard, in weight, or in measure.
LEVITICUS 19:35

A false balance is abomination to the LORD:
but a just weight is his delight.
PROVERBS 11:1

But thou shalt have a perfect and just weight,
a perfect and just measure shalt thou have:
that thy days may be lengthened in the land which the
LORD thy God giveth thee. For all that do such things,
and all that do unrighteously, are an
abomination unto the LORD thy God.
DEUTERONOMY 25:15–16

That no man go beyond and defraud his brother
in any matter: because that the Lord is the avenger of
all such, as we also have forewarned you and testified.
For God hath not called us unto uncleanness,
but unto holiness.

1 Thessalonians 4:6–7

Lie not one to another, seeing that ye have put
off the old man with his deeds; And have put
on the new man, which is renewed in knowledge
after the image of him that created him.

Colossians 3:9–10

*Lord, I know I am Your representative here on earth and
should give no one the opportunity to reject You because
of my actions. When I am within seconds of being a bad
example with my words, help me be honest instead. Amen.*

The wicked borroweth, and payeth not again:
but the righteous sheweth mercy, and giveth.

Psalm 37:21

Withhold not good from them to whom it is due,
when it is in the power of thine hand to do it.

Proverbs 3:27

And if thou sell ought unto thy neighbour,
or buyest ought of thy neighbour's hand,
ye shall not oppress one another.
LEVITICUS 25:14

Ye shall not therefore oppress one another; but thou
shalt fear thy God: for I am the LORD your God.
LEVITICUS 25:17

Father, exercising honesty is a challenge.
I ask You to give me power to govern
my thoughts and my words. Amen.

Better is a little with righteousness
than great revenues without right.
PROVERBS 16:8

He that walketh righteously, and speaketh uprightly;
he that despiseth the gain of oppressions, that shaketh
his hands from holding of bribes, that stoppeth his
ears from hearing of blood, and shutteth his
eyes from seeing evil; He shall dwell on high:
his place of defence shall be the munitions of rocks:
bread shall be given him; his waters shall be sure.
ISAIAH 33:15–16

HOPE

THOUGH AT TIMES we face severe trials, Christians should never lose hope. Our trust is in God—who will never fail us.

Lord, You are my hope in an often hopeless world. You are my hope of heaven, my hope of peace, my hope of change, purpose, and unconditional love. Fill the reservoir of my heart to overflowing with the joy that real hope brings. Amen.

Why art thou cast down, O my soul?
and why art thou disquieted within me?
hope thou in God: for I shall yet praise him,
who is the health of my countenance, and my God.
PSALM 42:11

Who by him do believe in God, that raised
him up from the dead, and gave him glory;
that your faith and hope might be in God.
1 PETER 1:21

Wherefore gird up the loins of your mind, be sober,
and hope to the end for the grace that is to be brought
unto you at the revelation of Jesus Christ.
1 PETER 1:13

And every man that hath this hope in him
purifieth himself, even as he is pure.
1 JOHN 3:3

The wicked is driven away in his wickedness:
but the righteous hath hope in his death.
PROVERBS 14:32

For the hope which is laid up for you in heaven,
whereof ye heard before in the word
of the truth of the gospel.
COLOSSIANS 1:5

Which is Christ in you, the hope of glory.
COLOSSIANS 1:27

You are the only source of hope that will never fail.
Show me how to take what I know about
You in my mind and let it take root in my heart.
Then I will have a garden of hope. Amen.

Be of good courage, and he shall strengthen your
heart, all ye that hope in the LORD.
PSALM 31:24

For thou art my hope, O Lord GOD:
thou art my trust from my youth.
PSALM 71:5

Blessed be the God and Father of our Lord Jesus
Christ, which according to his abundant mercy
hath begotten us again unto a lively hope by the
resurrection of Jesus Christ from the dead.
1 PETER 1:3

HUMILITY

FOR MOST OF us, displaying humility goes against our nature. But Jesus Christ showed us the ultimate example of humility: Though He was fully God, as a man He submitted to the Father's plan when He was arrested, abused, and killed on the cross.

Whenever I feel pressure to exalt myself above others,
Lord, remind me that my worth is found in You alone.
Teach me to serve, to love, to be honest, to put the needs
of others first—to live a humble but blessed life. Amen.

Whosoever therefore shall humble himself as this little
child, the same is greatest in the kingdom of heaven.
MATTHEW 18:4

LORD, thou hast heard the desire of the humble:
thou wilt prepare their heart,
thou wilt cause thine ear to hear.
PSALM 10:17

And whosoever shall exalt himself shall be abased;
and he that shall humble himself shall be exalted.
MATTHEW 23:12

For thus saith the high and lofty One that inhabiteth
eternity, whose name is Holy; I dwell in the high and
holy place, with him also that is of a contrite and
humble spirit, to revive the spirit of the humble,
and to revive the heart of the contrite ones.
ISAIAH 57:15

Better it is to be of an humble spirit with the lowly,
than to divide the spoil with the proud.
PROVERBS 16:19

But he giveth more grace.
Wherefore he saith, God resisteth the proud,
but giveth grace unto the humble.
JAMES 4:6

When he maketh inquisition for blood,
he remembereth them: he forgetteth
not the cry of the humble.
PSALM 9:12

Help me to realize that humility and doing Your will should
come first, no matter what my present situation is.
Help me keep my eyes on You, heavenly Father,
and the rest will take care of itself. Amen.

By humility and the fear of the LORD are riches,
and honour, and life.
PROVERBS 22:4

Surely he scorneth the scorners:
but he giveth grace unto the lowly.
PROVERBS 3:34

The fear of the LORD is the instruction of wisdom;
and before honour is humility.
PROVERBS 15:33

A man's pride shall bring him low: but honour
shall uphold the humble in spirit.
PROVERBS 29:23

If pride has caused my troubles, show me where it lies in me.
Humble my heart before You, holy Father. Amen.

Humble yourselves therefore under the mighty hand
of God, that he may exalt you in due time.
1 PETER 5:6

....
....
....
....
....
....
....
....
....
....
....
....
....

JOY

JOY IS A key part of the Christian life, because knowing God brings security and delight in the Savior. No one experiences true joy without an intimate relationship with Him.

Only when my life is anchored in Your love will my joy endure regardless of the circumstances. And that's the kind of joy I want—steady and enduring. Thank You, Lord, for a heart full of divine joy. Amen.

For ye shall go out with joy, and be led forth
with peace: the mountains and the hills shall
break forth before you into singing, and
all the trees of the field shall clap their hands.
ISAIAH 55:12

Blessed is the people that know the joyful sound:
they shall walk, O LORD, in the light of thy
countenance. In thy name shall they rejoice all the day:
and in thy righteousness shall they be exalted.
PSALM 89:15–16

The voice of rejoicing and salvation is in the
tabernacles of the righteous: the right hand
of the LORD doeth valiantly.
PSALM 118:15

Thou hast put gladness in my heart, more than in the
time that their corn and their wine increased.
PSALM 4:7

They that sow in tears shall reap in joy.
He that goeth forth and weepeth, bearing precious
seed, shall doubtless come again with rejoicing,
bringing his sheaves with him.
PSALM 126:5–6

These things have I spoken unto you,
that my joy might remain in you,
and that your joy might be full.
JOHN 15:11

Thou wilt shew me the path of life:
in thy presence is fulness of joy;
at thy right hand there are pleasures for evermore.
PSALM 16:11

*Father, help me to offer an easy smile and an honest laugh
that encourages people to spend time in my presence.
I pray I will always have a joyful outlook that lightens
my life and the lives of those around me. Amen.*

Light is sown for the righteous, and gladness for the
upright in heart. Rejoice in the LORD, ye righteous;
and give thanks at the remembrance of his holiness.
PSALM 97:11–12

Yet I will rejoice in the LORD,
I will joy in the God of my salvation.
HABAKKUK 3:18

Therefore the redeemed of the LORD shall return, and come with singing unto Zion; and everlasting joy shall be upon their head: they shall obtain gladness and joy; and sorrow and mourning shall flee away.

ISAIAH 51:11

Thank You for this time of rejoicing, Lord. Following times of trial, I've begun to see the good goal You had in mind all along. Thank You, Lord, for guiding me on the way. Amen.

For our heart shall rejoice in him,
because we have trusted in his holy name.

PSALM 33:21

Whom having not seen, ye love; in whom,
though now ye see him not, yet believing,
ye rejoice with joy unspeakable and full of glory.

1 PETER 1:8

I will greatly rejoice in the LORD, my soul shall
be joyful in my God; for he hath clothed me
with the garments of salvation, he hath covered
me with the robe of righteousness, as a bridegroom
decketh himself with ornaments, and as
a bride adorneth herself with her jewels.

ISAIAH 61:10

Then he said unto them, Go your way, eat the fat,
and drink the sweet, and send portions unto them
for whom nothing is prepared: for this day is
holy unto our LORD: neither be ye sorry;
for the joy of the LORD is your strength.
NEHEMIAH 8:10

And thou shalt rejoice in the LORD,
and shalt glory in the Holy One of Israel.
ISAIAH 41:16

Please speak clearly to the deepest part of me.
Encourage me in a way that goes deeper than the words
of those who love me. Lift me out of this depression,
and restore my joy for living. Amen.

The righteous shall be glad in the LORD, and shall trust
in him; and all the upright in heart shall glory.
PSALM 64:10

My soul shall be satisfied as with marrow and fatness;
and my mouth shall praise thee with joyful lips.
PSALM 63:5

But let the righteous be glad; let them rejoice before
God: yea, let them exceedingly rejoice.
PSALM 68:3

LAZINESS

THERE'S A DIFFERENCE between resting and laziness. God commands us to rest—but strongly urges us to avoid the pitfalls of laziness.

Father, sometimes I become despondent. It is as if some of the light has gone out in my life. Help me face the challenges before me with boldness. Amen.

I went by the field of the slothful, and by the vineyard of the man void of understanding; And, lo, it was all grown over with thorns, and nettles had covered the face thereof, and the stone wall thereof was broken down. Then I saw, and considered it well: I looked upon it, and received instruction. Yet a little sleep, a little slumber, a little folding of the hands to sleep: So shall thy poverty come as one that travelleth; and thy want as an armed man.

PROVERBS 24:30–34

Love not sleep, lest thou come to poverty; open thine eyes, and thou shalt be satisfied with bread.

PROVERBS 20:13

Lord, I ask You to show me the doors of opportunity that I can open to grow and improve. Jar me out of my routine and force me out of my comfort zone. Help me push beyond the mundane into the realm of active service. Amen.

The way of the slothful man is as an hedge of thorns: but the way of the righteous is made plain.

PROVERBS 15:19

Be thou diligent to know the state of thy flocks, and look well to thy herds.

PROVERBS 27:23

The thoughts of the diligent tend only to
plenteousness; but of every one
that is hasty only to want.
PROVERBS 21:5

The hand of the diligent shall bear rule:
but the slothful shall be under tribute.
PROVERBS 12:24

Let him that stole steal no more: but rather let
him labour, working with his hands the thing which
is good, that he may have to give to him that needeth.
EPHESIANS 4:28

Father, often it is easy to agree if the agreement is to do
nothing. Let my agreement be to act and do,
not sit back and wait. Amen.

He that tilleth his land shall be satisfied with bread:
but he that followeth vain persons
is void of understanding.
PROVERBS 12:11

And thou shalt have goats' milk enough for thy
food, for the food of thy household, and for the
maintenance for thy maidens.
PROVERBS 27:27

Behold that which I have seen: it is good
and comely for one to eat and to drink,
and to enjoy the good of all his labour
that he taketh under the sun all the days of his life,
which God giveth him: for it is his portion.
Every man also to whom God hath given riches
and wealth, and hath given him power to eat thereof,
and to take his portion, and to rejoice
in his labour; this is the gift of God.
ECCLESIASTES 5:18–19

LONELINESS

THE LORD MADE people to have relationships—both with Himself and with others. God recognizes and provides for our need for companionship. His best prescription for loneliness: relationships with Himself and His people.

Thank You for caring for my loneliness and giving me a defense against it. I'm so glad to be part of Your family. But most of all, Father, I am proud to be Your child. Amen.

I will not leave you comfortless:
I will come to you.
JOHN 14:18

Then shalt thou call, and the LORD shall answer;
thou shalt cry, and he shall say, Here I am.
ISAIAH 58:9

Since thou wast precious in my sight, thou hast been
honourable, and I have loved thee.
ISAIAH 43:4

And will be a Father unto you, and ye shall be my sons
and daughters, saith the Lord Almighty.
2 CORINTHIANS 6:18

*You don't just notice me and pass on—You actually take the
time to think about me, pay attention to me, help me when
I need help, and protect me when I need protecting. I am not
alone. I am not forsaken. Thank You, Lord. Amen.*

And, behold, I am with thee, and will keep thee in all
places whither thou goest, and will bring thee again
into this land; for I will not leave thee, until I have
done that which I have spoken to thee of.
GENESIS 28:15

LONG LIFE

THESE DAYS, IT'S not unusual for people to live well into their eighties—or even beyond. And though God doesn't promise long life to everyone, He has vowed always to remain faithful to us—however long we have on earth, then in His presence above.

I thank You, Father God, for the many years You have given
me and ask that You be with me when my time is up.
Thank You for a long, productive life and
that my time is in Your hands. Amen.

And even to your old age I am he; and even to hoar
hairs will I carry you: I have made, and I will bear;
even I will carry, and will deliver you.

ISAIAH 46:4

With the ancient is wisdom; and in length of days
understanding. With him is wisdom and strength,
he hath counsel and understanding.

JOB 12:12–13

The glory of young men is their strength:
and the beauty of old men is the grey head.

PROVERBS 20:29

*Thank You, Father, for Your help, support, and provision
as I age. May I use these years to glorify Your love,
so that my life will serve as an example to younger
generations of Your strength and care. Amen.*

Children's children are the crown of old men;
and the glory of children are their fathers.

PROVERBS 17:6

The hoary head is a crown of glory,
if it be found in the way of righteousness.

PROVERBS 16:31

And thine age shall be clearer than the noonday:
thou shalt shine forth, thou shalt be as the morning.
JOB 11:17

My son, forget not my law; but let thine heart keep my
commandments: For length of days, and long life,
and peace, shall they add to thee.
PROVERBS 3:1–2

Cast me not off in the time of old age;
forsake me not when my strength faileth.
PSALM 71:9

But speak thou the things which become sound
doctrine: That the aged men be sober, grave,
temperate, sound in faith, in charity, in patience.
The aged women likewise, that they be in behaviour
as becometh holiness, not false accusers,
not given to much wine, teachers of good things;
That they may teach the young women to be sober,
to love their husbands, to love their children,
To be discreet, chaste, keepers at home, good,
obedient to their own husbands,
that the word of God be not blasphemed.
TITUS 2:1–5

O God, thou hast taught me from my youth:
and hitherto have I declared thy wondrous works.
Now also when I am old and greyheaded,
O God, forsake me not; until I have shewed
thy strength unto this generation, and
thy power to every one that is to come.
PSALM 71:17–18

*A long lifetime of experience brings wisdom that should
be shared. Keep my heart young and my spirit strong,
Father, so I may do Your work throughout my life. Amen.*

LORD, make me to know mine end, and the measure
of my days, what it is: that I may know how frail I am.
Behold, thou hast made my days as an handbreadth;
and mine age is as nothing before thee.
PSALM 39:4–5

Ye shall walk in all the ways which the LORD your God
hath commanded you, that ye may live, and that it
may be well with you, and that ye may prolong
your days in the land which ye shall possess.
DEUTERONOMY 5:33

With long life will I satisfy him,
and shew him my salvation.
PSALM 91:16

That thou mightest fear the LORD thy God,
to keep all his statutes and his commandments,
which I command thee, thou, and thy son,
and thy son's son, all the days of thy life;
and that thy days may be prolonged.
DEUTERONOMY 6:2

*When I grow old, Lord, I pray that I will see the fruits of my
labor and rejoice, knowing that all my efforts were well worth
the time and energy I put into them. Amen.*

The fear of the LORD prolongeth days:
but the years of the wicked shall be shortened.
PROVERBS 10:27

For by me thy days shall be multiplied,
and the years of thy life shall be increased.
PROVERBS 9:11

LOVE, BROTHERLY

ONE OF THE Christian's greatest challenges is loving others. People, after all, cause us pain, even when they don't mean to. Let's face it—loving others can be a real sacrifice. But it's a sacrifice Jesus calls us to make in *His* strength. When we can't seem to obey, He will help us to love.

Lord, in Your generous, gracious love, You cared for me, even when I ignored You. Help me to love others as You loved me. I want to be part of Your mission to open blind eyes and raise bowed-down hearts. Amen.

A new commandment I give unto you, That ye love one another; as I have loved you, that ye also love one another. By this shall all men know that ye are my disciples, if ye have love one to another.

JOHN 13:34–35

Let love be without dissimulation. Abhor that which is evil; cleave to that which is good. Be kindly affectioned one to another with brotherly love; in honour preferring one another.

ROMANS 12:9–10

I know I can't love on my own, Lord, but through Your Spirit I can do all things—even this. When I seek to love others, I need to keep my eyes on You. Sweep away my critical attitude, and fill me with Your love. Amen.

But as touching brotherly love ye need not that I write unto you: for ye yourselves are taught of God to love one another.

1 THESSALONIANS 4:9

He that loveth his brother abideth in the light, and there is none occasion of stumbling in him.

1 JOHN 2:10

Seeing ye have purified your souls in obeying
the truth through the Spirit unto unfeigned
love of the brethren, see that ye love one
another with a pure heart fervently.
1 PETER 1:22

My little children, let us not love in word,
neither in tongue; but in deed and in truth.
1 JOHN 3:18

Beloved, if God so loved us,
we ought also to love one another.
1 JOHN 4:11

Beloved, let us love one another: for love is of God;
and every one that loveth is born of God,
and knoweth God. He that loveth not
knoweth not God; for God is love.
1 JOHN 4:7–8

Put on therefore, as the elect of God, holy and beloved,
bowels of mercies, kindness, humbleness of mind,
meekness, longsuffering; Forbearing one another,
and forgiving one another, if any man
have a quarrel against any: even as
Christ forgave you, so also do ye.
COLOSSIANS 3:12–13

LOVE, GOD'S

EVERY PAGE OF God's Word proclaims His love for us. The key message of the Bible is that, when humanity turned from Him, our Lord chose to take that sin on Himself rather than accept the broken relationship that resulted from human disobedience. What more could He do for us?

Forgive me for my double-mindedness, Lord.
Yours is a wonderful love that does not count wrongs.
Help me live in that love every day. Amen.

For God so loved the world, that he gave
his only begotten Son, that whosoever believeth
in him should not perish, but have everlasting life.
JOHN 3:16

And he will love thee, and bless thee, and multiply
thee: he will also bless the fruit of thy womb, and the
fruit of thy land, thy corn, and thy wine, and thine oil,
the increase of thy kine, and the flocks of thy sheep, in
the land which he sware unto thy fathers to give thee.
DEUTERONOMY 7:13

The LORD openeth the eyes of the blind:
the LORD raiseth them that are bowed down:
the LORD loveth the righteous.
PSALM 146:8

The way of the wicked is an abomination
unto the LORD: but he loveth him that
followeth after righteousness.
PROVERBS 15:9

For as a young man marrieth a virgin, so shall
thy sons marry thee: and as the bridegroom rejoiceth
over the bride, so shall thy God rejoice over thee.
ISAIAH 62:5

Herein is love, not that we loved God,
but that he loved us, and sent his Son
to be the propitiation for our sins.
1 JOHN 4:10

I will heal their backsliding, I will love them freely:
for mine anger is turned away from him.
HOSEA 14:4

The LORD thy God in the midst of thee is mighty;
he will save, he will rejoice over thee with joy; he will
rest in his love, he will joy over thee with singing.
ZEPHANIAH 3:17

You have promised that those who love are born of You.
Bring Your love into each relationship I have, Father, and
let it be a testimony to Your ability to bring love into humble
human lives. Fill my life with Your reaching-out love. Amen.

The LORD hath appeared of old unto me, saying,
Yea, I have loved thee with an everlasting love:
therefore with lovingkindness have I drawn thee.
JEREMIAH 31:3

Yea, I will rejoice over them to do them good,
and I will plant them in this land assuredly with
my whole heart and with my whole soul.
JEREMIAH 32:41

But God, who is rich in mercy,
for his great love wherewith he loved us,
Even when we were dead in sins, hath quickened
us together with Christ, (by grace ye are saved;) And
hath raised us up together, and made us sit together
in heavenly places in Christ Jesus: That in the ages to
come he might shew the exceeding riches of his grace
in his kindness toward us through Christ Jesus.
EPHESIANS 2:4–7

*Keep me trusting in You, Lord, aware that You have not left
me by the side of the road. I want to reflect Your love
and faithfulness every moment of my life. Amen.*

And we have known and believed the love that
God hath to us. God is love; and he that dwelleth
in love dwelleth in God, and God in him.
1 JOHN 4:16

For the Father himself loveth you, because ye have
loved me, and have believed that I came out from God.
JOHN 16:27

We love him, because he first loved us.
1 JOHN 4:19

And I have declared unto them thy name,
and will declare it: that the love wherewith
thou hast loved me may be in them, and I in them.
JOHN 17:26

Father, I need to feel Your love. Draw me close.
Hold me in Your arms like a little child.
Let Your love wash over me like tears of joy. Amen.

I in them, and thou in me, that they may be
made perfect in one; and that the world may know
that thou hast sent me, and hast loved them,
as thou hast loved me.
JOHN 17:23

Now our Lord Jesus Christ himself, and God,
even our Father, which hath loved us,
and hath given us everlasting consolation
and good hope through grace, Comfort your hearts,
and stablish you in every good word and work.
2 THESSALONIANS 2:16–17

LOVING GOD

WHEN WE REALLY consider the breadth and depth of God's love for us, we might be overwhelmed. He loves us freely, without reservation. How can you reciprocate that love today? Talk to God. Praise Him. Seek His presence. Share Him with a friend. Live in His love. There are countless ways to love God.

Father, as I start each day, I want to give You thanks and praise. More than anything else, I want to acknowledge who You are. You are the reason I get up each morning. Amen.

Know therefore that the LORD thy God, he is God,
the faithful God, which keepeth covenant
and mercy with them that love him and keep
his commandments to a thousand generations.
DEUTERONOMY 7:9

I love them that love me;
and those that seek me early shall find me.
PROVERBS 8:17

He that hath my commandments, and keepeth them,
he it is that loveth me: and he that loveth me shall
be loved of my Father, and I will love him,
and will manifest myself to him.
JOHN 14:21

*Lord, I don't know if I'll ever understand why You sacrificed
Yourself for me. But, from the depths of my being,
I want to shout praise to You. Amen.*

That I may cause those that love me to inherit
substance; and I will fill their treasures.
PROVERBS 8:21

Delight thyself also in the LORD:
and he shall give thee the desires of thine heart.
PSALM 37:4

Because he hath set his love upon me,
therefore will I deliver him: I will set him on high,
because he hath known my name.
PSALM 91:14

But as it is written, Eye hath not seen, nor ear heard,
neither have entered into the heart of man, the things
which God hath prepared for them that love him.
1 CORINTHIANS 2:9

The LORD preserveth all them that love him:
but all the wicked will he destroy.
PSALM 145:20

And it shall come to pass, if ye shall hearken
diligently unto my commandments which I command
you this day, to love the LORD your God, and to serve
him with all your heart and with all your soul,
That I will give you the rain of your land in his due
season, the first rain and the latter rain, that thou
mayest gather in thy corn, and thy wine, and thine oil.
And I will send grass in thy fields for thy cattle,
that thou mayest eat and be full.
DEUTERONOMY 11:13–15

Grace be with all them that love our
Lord Jesus Christ in sincerity. Amen.
EPHESIANS 6:24

LUST

WE OFTEN ASSOCIATE the word *lust* with a sexual desire outside of God's plan for our lives. But the truth is that when anything takes the place of God in our minds and hearts, we're experiencing lust.

Turn me from the lusts that focus my eyes on the temporary and keep them from You. Remind me that today's temptation and trials will seem small in the light of eternity. Amen.

✝

From whence come wars and fightings among you?
come they not hence, even of your lusts
that war in your members? Ye lust, and have not:
ye kill, and desire to have, and cannot obtain:
ye fight and war, yet ye have not, because ye ask not.
Ye ask, and receive not, because ye ask amiss,
that ye may consume it upon your lusts. Ye adulterers
and adulteresses, know ye not that the friendship
of the world is enmity with God? whosoever therefore
will be a friend of the world is the enemy of God.

JAMES 4:1–4

For all that is in the world, the lust of the flesh,
and the lust of the eyes, and the pride of life, is not of
the Father, but is of the world. And the world passeth
away, and the lust thereof: but he that doeth
the will of God abideth for ever.

1 JOHN 2:16–17

Ye have heard that it was said by them of old time,
Thou shalt not commit adultery: But I say unto you,
That whosoever looketh on a woman to lust after her
hath committed adultery with her already in his heart.

MATTHEW 5:27–28

Lust not after her beauty in thine heart;
neither let her take thee with her eyelids.
For by means of a whorish woman a man
is brought to a piece of bread: and
the adultress will hunt for the precious life.
Can a man take fire in his bosom,
and his clothes not be burned?
Can one go upon hot coals, and
his feet not be burned? So he that goeth
in to his neighbour's wife; whosoever
toucheth her shall not be innocent.
PROVERBS 6:25–29

Help me, Lord, to bring my temptations and sins to You.
Cleanse my heart and mind as I confess to You.
Fill my life with Your grace. Amen.

Submit yourselves therefore to God. Resist the devil,
and he will flee from you. Draw nigh to God,
and he will draw nigh to you. Cleanse your hands,
ye sinners; and purify your hearts, ye double minded.
JAMES 4:7–8

Dearly beloved, I beseech you as strangers and pilgrims,
abstain from fleshly lusts, which war against the soul.
1 PETER 2:11

They told you there should be mockers in the last time, who should walk after their own ungodly lusts. These be they who separate themselves, sensual, having not the Spirit. But ye, beloved, building up yourselves on your most holy faith, praying in the Holy Ghost, Keep yourselves in the love of God, looking for the mercy of our Lord Jesus Christ unto eternal life.

JUDE 18-21

Walk in the Spirit, and ye shall not fulfil the lust of the flesh. For the flesh lusteth against the Spirit, and the Spirit against the flesh: and these are contrary the one to the other: so that ye cannot do the things that ye would.

GALATIANS 5:16-17

Lord, I am human and often tempted.
Be with me when I am tempted and show me
the true joys of self-control. Amen.

Likewise reckon ye also yourselves to be dead indeed unto sin, but alive unto God through Jesus Christ our Lord. Let not sin therefore reign in your mortal body, that ye should obey it in the lusts thereof. For sin shall not have dominion over you: for ye are not under the law, but under grace.

ROMANS 6:11-12, 14

LYING

BECAUSE GOD IS always truthful, His people must be, too. But sin has so warped our being that we often give in to exaggeration, misleading words, even outright falsehoods. The good news is that when we take these inconsistencies to "the way, the *truth*, and the life" (John 14:6), asking His forgiveness, He will separate us from that sin.

I'm ashamed to admit that I often speak before I think, and the words that come out of my mouth are not always truthful. Help me to be wise enough to pause first, then strong enough to speak the truth. Amen.

Lie not one to another, seeing that ye have
put off the old man with his deeds;
And have put on the new man, which is renewed in
knowledge after the image of him that created him.
COLOSSIANS 3:9–10

And ye shall not swear by my name falsely,
neither shalt thou profane the name of thy God:
I am the LORD.
LEVITICUS 19:12

A man that beareth false witness against his neighbour
is a maul, and a sword, and a sharp arrow.
PROVERBS 25:18

*Father, Your Holy Spirit is telling me that being completely
truthful is not one of my strengths and I need
to work on it. Help me to turn things over to
You so I can speak with integrity. Amen.*

A faithful witness will not lie:
but a false witness will utter lies.
PROVERBS 14:5

Thou shalt not raise a false report:
put not thine hand with the wicked
to be an unrighteous witness.
EXODUS 23:1

A false witness shall not be unpunished,
and he that speaketh lies shall not escape.
PROVERBS 19:5

But the fearful, and unbelieving, and the abominable,
and murderers, and whoremongers, and sorcerers,
and idolaters, and all liars, shall have their part
in the lake which burneth with fire and brimstone:
which is the second death.
REVELATION 21:8

If a false witness rise up against any man to testify
against him that which is wrong; Then both the men,
between whom the controversy is, shall stand
before the LORD, before the priests and the judges,
which shall be in those days; And the judges shall
make diligent inquisition: and, behold, if the witness
be a false witness, and hath testified falsely against
his brother; Then shall ye do unto him, as he had
thought to have done unto his brother: so shalt
thou put the evil away from among you.
DEUTERONOMY 19:16-19

A false witness shall not be unpunished,
and he that speaketh lies shall perish.
PROVERBS 19:9

Be not a witness against thy neighbour without cause;
and deceive not with thy lips.
PROVERBS 24:28

O God, put words of kindness and truth in my mouth.
I desire to be virtuous. Amen.

The wicked are estranged from the womb:
they go astray as soon as they be born, speaking lies.
PSALM 58:3

But if ye have bitter envying and strife in your hearts,
glory not, and lie not against the truth.
JAMES 3:14

The lip of truth shall be established for ever:
but a lying tongue is but for a moment.
PROVERBS 12:19

MARRIAGE

MARRIAGE IS A picture of the relationship between God and His people. So, not surprisingly, God discourages marriage between believers and those who have no faith in Him. The marital relationship is a very special covenant between God and two people, to be honored by all. Partners are to remain faithful to each other for life.

Heavenly Father, thank You for the gift of marriage, for teaching my spouse and me what love really means by helping us work through a lifelong relationship. Amen.

Live joyfully with the wife whom thou lovest all the
days of the life of thy vanity, which he hath given thee
under the sun, all the days of thy vanity: for that
is thy portion in this life, and in thy labour
which thou takest under the sun.
ECCLESIASTES 9:9

Drink waters out of thine own cistern,
and running waters out of thine own well.
PROVERBS 5:15

Let thy fountain be blessed: and rejoice with the wife
of thy youth. Let her be as the loving hind and pleasant
roe; let her breasts satisfy thee at all times; and be thou
ravished always with her love. And why wilt thou,
my son, be ravished with a strange woman,
and embrace the bosom of a stranger?
PROVERBS 5:18–20

Let the husband render unto the wife due benevolence:
and likewise also the wife unto the husband.
1 CORINTHIANS 7:3

Wives, submit yourselves unto your own husbands,
as unto the Lord. For the husband is the head of the
wife, even as Christ is the head of the church:
and he is the saviour of the body.
EPHESIANS 5:22–23

Husbands, love your wives, even as Christ also loved
the church, and gave himself for it.
EPHESIANS 5:25

So ought men to love their wives as their own bodies.
He that loveth his wife loveth himself.
EPHESIANS 5:28

For this cause shall a man leave his father
and mother, and shall be joined unto his wife,
and they two shall be one flesh.
EPHESIANS 5:31

*I am thankful, Lord, that you set aside someone
for me to love. I pray that I will respect my spouse
as a faithful partner and that we may walk side
by side in the path You direct. Amen.*

Nevertheless let every one of you in particular
so love his wife even as himself; and the wife
see that she reverence her husband.
EPHESIANS 5:33

But if any provide not for his own, and specially
for those of his own house, he hath denied the faith,
and is worse than an infidel.
1 TIMOTHY 5:8

Wives, submit yourselves unto your own husbands,
as it is fit in the Lord. Husbands, love your wives,
and be not bitter against them.

COLOSSIANS 3:18–19

Likewise, ye husbands, dwell with them according
to knowledge, giving honour unto the wife, as unto
the weaker vessel, and as being heirs together of
the grace of life; that your prayers be not hindered.

1 PETER 3:7

*Father, teach me and my spouse to work as a team,
sharing the good times and the bad, so that neither
of us should be overburdened. Amen.*

That they may teach the young women to be sober,
to love their husbands, to love their children,
To be discreet, chaste, keepers at home,
good, obedient to their own husbands,
that the word of God be not blasphemed.

TITUS 2:4–5

MEEKNESS

DOES MEEKNESS EQUAL weakness? The world seems to think so, but Jesus says otherwise. He said the meek will be blessed. Why? Because when we check our own egos at the door, we are open to His teaching, to His correction, to His will. When we are meek, Jesus is strong!

Thank You, Lord, for offering grace in increasing amounts.
Encourage me in humility, that I may draw closer to you.
Amen.

Blessed are the meek: for they shall inherit the earth.
MATTHEW 5:5

But with righteousness shall he judge the poor,
and reprove with equity for the meek of the earth.
ISAIAH 11:4

The meek also shall increase their joy in the LORD,
and the poor among men shall rejoice
in the Holy One of Israel.
ISAIAH 29:19

*Many in this world might consider themselves
"nobodies"—the poor, the oppressed, the hardworking.
But they are made beautiful by their meek and quiet spirits.
Thank You, Lord, for showing me that every person
is a source of joy for You. Amen.*

The LORD lifteth up the meek: he casteth
the wicked down to the ground.
PSALM 147:6

The meek will he guide in judgment:
and the meek will he teach his way.
PSALM 25:9

But the meek shall inherit the earth;
and shall delight themselves
in the abundance of peace.
PSALM 37:11

A soft answer turneth away wrath:
but grievous words stir up anger.
PROVERBS 15:1

Seek ye the LORD, all ye meek of the earth,
which have wrought his judgment; seek righteousness,
seek meekness: it may be ye shall be hid in
the day of the LORD's anger.
ZEPHANIAH 2:3

But let it be the hidden man of the heart,
in that which is not corruptible, even the ornament
of a meek and quiet spirit, which is in
the sight of God of great price.
1 PETER 3:4

The meek shall eat and be satisfied:
they shall praise the LORD that seek him:
your heart shall live for ever.
PSALM 22:26

MERCY

LEFT TO OURSELVES, we are engulfed by sin. But God mercifully sent His Son to die for every wrong thought and deed. As we draw near to Him in faith, our understanding of His mercy grows. We recognize our own deep need for Him in every corner of our lives, and we begin to respond to His love by living mercifully with others.

When I sin, I experience pain, but You, Lord, do not leave me there. Suffering lasts for a while, but it is not Your final goal for me. Mercy is. Pour Your mercy out on my life, and help me share it with others. Amen.

And therefore will the LORD wait, that he may be
gracious unto you, and therefore will he be exalted,
that he may have mercy upon you:
for the LORD is a God of judgment:
blessed are all they that wait for him.
ISAIAH 30:18

And the LORD passed by before him, and proclaimed,
The LORD, The LORD God, merciful and gracious,
longsuffering, and abundant in goodness and truth,
Keeping mercy for thousands, forgiving iniquity
and transgression and sin, and that will by no means
clear the guilty; visiting the iniquity of the fathers upon
the children, and upon the children's children,
unto the third and to the fourth generation.
EXODUS 34:6–7

Like as a father pitieth his children,
so the LORD pitieth them that fear him.
PSALM 103:13

But the mercy of the LORD is from everlasting
to everlasting upon them that fear him,
and his righteousness unto children's children.
PSALM 103:17

And he said, I will make all my goodness pass before thee, and I will proclaim the name of the LORD before thee; and will be gracious to whom I will be gracious, and will shew mercy on whom I will shew mercy.
EXODUS 33:19

Thank You for caring for me when I wallowed in sin. I did nothing to earn Your grace, yet You gave it to me anyway. May Your great mercy be reflected in my life, Lord, as I pass on mercy to those who sin against me. May mercy flow freely in my life. Amen.

And I will have mercy upon her that had not obtained mercy; and I will say to them which were not my people, Thou art my people; and they shall say, Thou art my God.
HOSEA 2:23

For in my wrath I smote thee, but in my favour have I had mercy on thee.
ISAIAH 60:10

For my name's sake will I defer mine anger, and for my praise will I refrain for thee, that I cut thee not off.
ISAIAH 48:9

MONEY

IT'S EASY TO forget that *everything* we have comes from God, even our finances. Not only does He give us money and things, God also promises that He will always provide for us. If we manage His gifts well as we follow Him, we will never lack what we need.

Father, when it comes to money matters,
I cannot approach perfection, but I know with
Your help I can learn to handle finances faithfully. Amen.

The sleep of a labouring man is sweet, whether
he eat little or much: but the abundance of the rich
will not suffer him to sleep. There is a sore evil
which I have seen under the sun, namely, riches kept
for the owners thereof to their hurt. But those riches
perish by evil travail: and he begetteth a son,
and there is nothing in his hand.

ECCLESIASTES 5:12–14

*When You bless me with money, make me generous, too,
Lord. I need to trust in Your provision. Be in charge
of my wallet and my life. Amen.*

But thou shalt remember the LORD thy God:
for it is he that giveth thee power to get wealth,
that he may establish his covenant which
he sware unto thy fathers, as it is this day.

DEUTERONOMY 8:18

Better is little with the fear of the LORD than
great treasure and trouble therewith.

PROVERBS 15:16

The rich and poor meet together:
the LORD is the maker of them all.

PROVERBS 22:2

For the needy shall not always be forgotten:
the expectation of the poor shall not perish for ever.
PSALM 9:18

He that trusteth in his riches shall fall:
but the righteous shall flourish as a branch.
PROVERBS 11:28

Remind me of Your blessings that have little to do with wealth: love, peace, good health, and the work of the Spirit in my life. Remind me, Lord, of the great cost of my salvation, and let me praise You forever. Amen.

A faithful man shall abound with blessings: but
he that maketh haste to be rich shall not be innocent.
PROVERBS 28:20

Riches profit not in the day of wrath:
but righteousness delivereth from death.
PROVERBS 11:4

They shall cast their silver in the streets,
and their gold shall be removed: their silver and their
gold shall not be able to deliver them in the day of the
wrath of the LORD: they shall not satisfy their souls,
neither fill their bowels: because it is
the stumblingblock of their iniquity.
EZEKIEL 7:19

There is that maketh himself rich, yet hath nothing:
there is that maketh himself poor, yet hath great riches.
PROVERBS 13:7

He that loveth silver shall not be satisfied
with silver; nor he that loveth abundance
with increase: this is also vanity.
ECCLESIASTES 5:10

*You've taken care of me and kept me going even in rough
times. Thank You, Father, for the spiritual and financial
wealth You've given me. I want to use it to Your glory. Amen.*

He that oppresseth the poor to increase his riches, and
he that giveth to the rich, shall surely come to want.
PROVERBS 22:16

He that hasteth to be rich hath an evil eye,
and considereth not that poverty shall come upon him.
PROVERBS 28:22

For we brought nothing into this world,
and it is certain we can carry nothing out.
1 TIMOTHY 6:7

Better is the poor that walketh in his uprightness,
than he that is perverse in his ways, though he be rich.
PROVERBS 28:6

Obedience

WERE YOU AN obedient child? Did you always obey when a parent told you to do (or avoid) something? Even the most well-behaved kid has moments of disobedience—and we're the same way as children of God. But as we mature and grow closer to the Father, we gain a wider understanding of why God commands what He does. . . and we more naturally and regularly obey Him.

Fill me with Your Spirit, Lord, so that I may glorify
You in every choice I make. Give me strength to obey
You completely, so each second of my days may be
filled with testimony to You. Amen.

See, I have set before thee this day life and good,
and death and evil; In that I command thee this day
to love the Lord thy God, to walk in his ways, and
to keep his commandments and his statutes and his
judgments, that thou mayest live and multiply:
and the Lord thy God shall bless thee in the
land whither thou goest to possess it.

Deuteronomy 30:15–16

And thou shalt do that which is right and good in the
sight of the Lord: that it may be well with thee,
and that thou mayest go in and possess the good
land which the Lord sware unto thy fathers.

Deuteronomy 6:18

Hear therefore, O Israel, and observe to do it; that
it may be well with thee, and that ye may increase
mightily, as the Lord God of thy fathers hath promised
thee, in the land that floweth with milk and honey.

Deuteronomy 6:3

Wherefore it shall come to pass, if ye hearken to these
judgments, and keep, and do them, that the Lord
thy God shall keep unto thee the covenant and
the mercy which he sware unto thy fathers.

Deuteronomy 7:12

Keep therefore the words of this covenant,
and do them, that ye may prosper in all that ye do.
DEUTERONOMY 29:9

O that there were such an heart in them, that they
would fear me, and keep all my commandments
always, that it might be well with them,
and with their children for ever!
DEUTERONOMY 5:29

Keep me obedient to Your love, Lord.
Help me trust that You will bring me good things.
I need faith to see blessings instead of fears. Amen.

Those things, which ye have both learned,
and received, and heard, and seen in me, do:
and the God of peace shall be with you.
PHILIPPIANS 4:9

Whosoever therefore shall break one of these least
commandments, and shall teach men so, he shall
be called the least in the kingdom of heaven:
but whosoever shall do and teach them, the same
shall be called great in the kingdom of heaven.
MATTHEW 5:19

Therefore whosoever heareth these sayings of
mine, and doeth them, I will liken him unto a
wise man, which built his house upon a rock:
And the rain descended, and the floods came,
and the winds blew, and beat upon that house;
and it fell not: for it was founded upon a rock.

MATTHEW 7:24–25

Jesus answered and said unto him, If a man love me,
he will keep my words: and my Father will love him,
and we will come unto him, and
make our abode with him.

JOHN 14:23

*I know I can't obey You all on my own, Lord. When I try,
I just get tied up in all the good I want to do. Make my heart
all Yours, and I will no longer struggle with sin. When my
soul prospers, surely my life will be blessed. Amen.*

And we know that all things work together
for good to them that love God, to them who
are the called according to his purpose.

ROMANS 8:28

If ye know these things, happy are ye if ye do them.

JOHN 13:17

If ye keep my commandments, ye shall abide
in my love; even as I have kept my Father's
commandments, and abide in his love.
JOHN 15:10

But whoso looketh into the perfect law of liberty,
and continueth therein, he being not
a forgetful hearer, but a doer of the work,
this man shall be blessed in his deed.
JAMES 1:25

For not the hearers of the law are just before God,
but the doers of the law shall be justified.
ROMANS 2:13

*Thank You, Father God, for the fruit You have given me
through the years. When I live to serve You through worship
and obedience, I do not wither or faint. Amen.*

Verily, verily, I say unto you, He that heareth my word,
and believeth on him that sent me, hath everlasting
life, and shall not come into condemnation;
but is passed from death unto life.
JOHN 5:24

For whosoever shall do the will of my Father which is in
heaven, the same is my brother, and sister, and mother.
MATTHEW 12:50

And the world passeth away, and the lust thereof:
but he that doeth the will of God abideth for ever.
1 JOHN 2:17

Not every one that saith unto me, Lord, Lord,
shall enter into the kingdom of heaven; but
he that doeth the will of my Father which is in heaven.
MATTHEW 7:21

And whatsoever we ask, we receive of him,
because we keep his commandments, and do
those things that are pleasing in his sight.
1 JOHN 3:22

PATICIENCE

PATIENCE IS ONE of those virtues many of us would like to avoid. We rush about, trying to complete as many tasks as possible, while patience is shoved off to one side. Just think how our impatience affects the other people in our lives! Often, God will force patience on us. It can be a hard lesson to learn, but we'd be pretty poor Christians if we never learned to wait patiently for His will.

I want to learn the benefit of patience,
Lord, without the struggles. Change my heart to wait
on You quietly and without complaint, so that
I will be ready for Your coming. Amen.

Be patient therefore, brethren, unto the coming of
the Lord. Behold, the husbandman waiteth for the
precious fruit of the earth, and hath long patience
for it, until he receive the early and latter rain.
Be ye also patient; stablish your hearts:
for the coming of the Lord draweth nigh.
JAMES 5:7–8

For what glory is it, if, when ye be buffeted for your
faults, ye shall take it patiently? but if, when ye do well,
and suffer for it, ye take it patiently,
this is acceptable with God.
1 PETER 2:20

And let us not be weary in well doing:
for in due season we shall reap, if we faint not.
GALATIANS 6:9

Let us hold fast the profession of our faith without
wavering; (for he is faithful that promised).
HEBREWS 10:23

But he that shall endure unto the end,
the same shall be saved.
MATTHEW 24:13

That ye be not slothful, but followers of them who
through faith and patience inherit the promises.
HEBREWS 6:12

For ye have need of patience, that, after ye have done
the will of God, ye might receive the promise.
HEBREWS 10:36

Forgive my impatience, Lord.
Some days I feel I will never get there, never see
Your promises fulfilled. Be patient with me. Amen.

My brethren, count it all joy when ye fall into divers
temptations; Knowing this, that the trying of your
faith worketh patience. But let patience have
her perfect work, that ye may be perfect
and entire, wanting nothing.
JAMES 1:2–4

And not only so, but we glory in tribulations also:
knowing that tribulation worketh patience;
And patience, experience; and experience, hope.
ROMANS 5:3–4

PEACE

MUCH AS WE seek peace in our lives, we cannot find the real thing until we have peace with God, who is the source of all peace. Real spiritual peace comes only through the Savior.

Heavenly Father, when life seems to be getting rough, I pray and the path becomes smooth before me. Thank You for Your peace, which goes before me every day. Amen.

Peace, peace to him that is far off, and to him
that is near, saith the LORD; and I will heal him.
ISAIAH 57:19

And let the peace of God rule in your hearts,
to the which also ye are called in one body;
and be ye thankful.
COLOSSIANS 3:15

*Father, help me to cling more tightly to You
than to my problems. I want to know the peace
that comes only from drawing close to Your side,
minute by minute, day by day. Amen.*

I will hear what God the LORD will speak: for he will
speak peace unto his people, and to his saints.
PSALM 85:8

And the peace of God, which passeth all
understanding, shall keep your hearts
and minds through Christ Jesus.
PHILIPPIANS 4:7

And the work of righteousness shall be peace;
and the effect of righteousness quietness
and assurance for ever.
ISAIAH 32:17

Thy faith hath saved thee; go in peace.
LUKE 7:50

Mark the perfect man, and behold the upright:
for the end of that man is peace.
PSALM 37:37

Now the Lord of peace himself give you
peace always by all means.
2 THESSALONIANS 3:16

Peace I leave with you, my peace I give unto you:
not as the world giveth, give I unto you.
Let not your heart be troubled, neither let it be afraid.
JOHN 14:27

PRAYER

Since it is communication with our Lord, prayer should be a precious thing. But how often do we skimp on prayer, pushing it out of our busy lives? Prayerless Christians become weak, helpless believers. But through faith-filled prayer, we can move mountains.

Father, I pray that during my life,
I can become one with You. I pray that I can talk with
You easily and often because it has become my nature. Amen.

Ask, and it shall be given you; seek, and ye shall find;
knock, and it shall be opened unto you: For every one
that asketh receiveth; and he that seeketh findeth;
and to him that knocketh it shall be opened.
MATTHEW 7:7–8

And all things, whatsoever ye shall ask in prayer,
believing, ye shall receive.
MATTHEW 21:22

He will be very gracious unto thee at the voice of thy
cry; when he shall hear it, he will answer thee.
ISAIAH 30:19

*Even when I have no special needs or requests and just want
to praise You for all Your blessings, I have a hard time finding
the right words. Thank You, Lord, for Your Holy Spirit
who intercedes on my behalf. Amen.*

And this is the confidence that we have in him, that,
if we ask any thing according to his will, he heareth us:
And if we know that he hear us, whatsoever we ask, we
know that we have the petitions that we desired of him.
1 JOHN 5:14–15

And it shall come to pass, that before they call, I will
answer; and while they are yet speaking, I will hear.
ISAIAH 65:24

Whatsoever ye shall ask the Father in my name,
he will give it you. Hitherto have ye asked
nothing in my name: ask, and ye shall receive,
that your joy may be full.

JOHN 16:23–24

Confess your faults one to another, and pray one for
another, that ye may be healed. The effectual fervent
prayer of a righteous man availeth much.

JAMES 5:16

*Father, I pray that I may always enter Your presence
in the proper way. I resolve to acknowledge with thanksgiving
what You have done for me. You are merciful, long-suffering,
and mindful of me. I praise You for the blessings
that flow from You. Amen.*

And I say unto you, Ask, and it shall be given you;
seek, and ye shall find; knock,
and it shall be opened unto you.

LUKE 11:9

And whatsoever ye shall ask in my name, that will I do,
that the Father may be glorified in the Son.
If ye shall ask any thing in my name, I will do it.

JOHN 14:13–14

If ye abide in me, and my words abide in you,
ye shall ask what ye will, and it shall be done unto you.
JOHN 15:7

But thou, when thou prayest, enter into thy closet,
and when thou hast shut thy door, pray to thy
Father which is in secret; and thy Father which
seeth in secret shall reward thee openly.
MATTHEW 6:6

He shall call upon me, and I will answer him.
PSALM 91:15

*I am thankful, Father, that I can talk to You day or night
about the things that trouble me. It is a comfort
to know that You are there to listen. Amen.*

The LORD is far from the wicked: but he heareth
the prayer of the righteous.
PROVERBS 15:29

O thou that hearest prayer,
unto thee shall all flesh come.
PSALM 65:2

The righteous cry, and the LORD heareth,
and delivereth them out of all their troubles.
PSALM 34:17

If ye then, being evil, know how to give
good gifts unto your children, how much
more shall your Father which is in heaven
give good things to them that ask him?
MATTHEW 7:11

Then shalt thou call, and the LORD shall answer;
thou shalt cry, and he shall say, Here I am.
ISAIAH 58:9

*Father, I thank You for answers to prayers. It is wonderful to
know I have a God who delights in hearing and answering
my prayers. I am glad to be able to give thanks. Amen.*

Evening, and morning, and at noon, will I pray,
and cry aloud: and he shall hear my voice.
PSALM 55:17

The LORD is nigh unto all them that call upon
him, to all that call upon him in truth.
He will fulfil the desire of them that fear him:
he also will hear their cry, and will save them.
PSALM 145:18–19

Then shall ye call upon me, and ye shall go
and pray unto me, and I will hearken unto you.
JEREMIAH 29:12

And I will bring the third part through the fire,
and will refine them as silver is refined,
and will try them as gold is tried: they shall call
on my name, and I will hear them: I will say,
It is my people: and they shall say,
The Lord is my God.
ZECHARIAH 13:9

Be not ye therefore like unto them:
for your Father knoweth what things
ye have need of, before ye ask him.
MATTHEW 6:8

And whatsoever we ask, we receive of him,
because we keep his commandments,
and do those things that are pleasing in his sight.
1 JOHN 3:22

PRIDE

PRIDE IS A dangerous sin that separates us from our all-powerful God. It was pride that caused Satan's fall, and ruined the perfect world God had created for humanity. When we focus on our own frail "power," we cannot truly see God as Lord.

Heavenly Father, we live in a world that lifts up proud people. Make us all aware of how much You value sacrifice. Help me to have the humble spirit I need when I come before You. Amen.

Pride goeth before destruction,
and an haughty spirit before a fall.
PROVERBS 16:18

Woe unto them that are wise in their own eyes,
and prudent in their own sight!
ISAIAH 5:21

Seest thou a man wise in his own conceit?
there is more hope of a fool than of him.
PROVERBS 26:12

*Don't let my pride keep me from freedom, Lord. Help me to
avoid temptation when it is still very small. Thank You
for being an escape hatch that is constantly available. Amen.*

Look on every one that is proud, and bring him low;
and tread down the wicked in their place.
JOB 40:12

An high look, and a proud heart,
and the plowing of the wicked, is sin.
PROVERBS 21:4

The fear of the LORD is to hate evil:
pride, and arrogancy, and the evil way,
and the froward mouth, do I hate.
PROVERBS 8:13

But he that glorieth, let him glory in the Lord.
For not he that commendeth himself approved,
but whom the Lord commendeth.
2 CORINTHIANS 10:17–18

And he said unto them, Ye are they which justify
yourselves before men; but God knoweth your hearts:
for that which is highly esteemed among men is
abomination in the sight of God.
LUKE 16:15

Let another man praise thee, and not thine own
mouth; a stranger, and not thine own lips.
PROVERBS 27:2

*Father, please help me remember that the greatest in the
kingdom of heaven is not the one being served, but the
humble one doing the serving. Amen.*

Thou hast rebuked the proud that are cursed,
which do err from thy commandments.
PSALM 119:21

He that is of a proud heart stirreth up strife: but he
that putteth his trust in the LORD shall be made fat.
He that trusteth in his own heart is a fool: but whoso
walketh wisely, he shall be delivered.
PROVERBS 28:25–26

PROTECTION, GOD'S

HAVE YOU EVER been protected from a close call, a rescue that you could only attribute to your guardian angel? God's protective care is all around us, whether we're aware of it or not.

Thank You, Lord, for being my Protector, no matter what situation I find myself in. Deliver me from all that binds me. Amen.

The name of the LORD is a strong tower:
the righteous runneth into it, and is safe.
PROVERBS 18:10

The angel of the LORD encampeth round about them
that fear him, and delivereth them.
PSALM 34:7

For the eyes of the LORD run to and fro throughout
the whole earth, to shew himself strong in the
behalf of them whose heart is perfect toward him.
Herein thou hast done foolishly: therefore from
henceforth thou shalt have wars.
2 CHRONICLES 16:9

The LORD shall preserve thee from all evil:
he shall preserve thy soul. The LORD shall
preserve thy going out and thy coming in
from this time forth, and even for evermore.
PSALM 121:7–8

When thou liest down, thou shalt not be afraid:
yea, thou shalt lie down, and thy sleep shall be sweet.
PROVERBS 3:24

And who is he that will harm you,
if ye be followers of that which is good?
1 PETER 3:13

The beloved of the LORD shall dwell in safety by him;
and the Lord shall cover him all the day long,
and he shall dwell between his shoulders.
DEUTERONOMY 33:12

*Often my foundation is undependable,
and it can send my life tumbling down after one bad storm.
Teach me to ground my life on You, Lord, the only Rock
who will stand forever against any storm. Amen.*

He shall not be afraid of evil tidings:
his heart is fixed, trusting in the LORD.
PSALM 112:7

Because thou hast made the LORD,
which is my refuge, even the most High,
thy habitation; There shall no evil befall thee,
neither shall any plague come nigh thy dwelling.
PSALM 91:9–10

But now thus saith the LORD that created thee,
O Jacob, and he that formed thee, O Israel, Fear not:
for I have redeemed thee, I have called thee by thy
name; thou art mine. When thou passest through
the waters, I will be with thee; and through the rivers,
they shall not overflow thee: when thou walkest
through the fire, thou shalt not be burned;
neither shall the flame kindle upon thee.

ISAIAH 43:1–2

Although I cannot physically touch Your hand in times of
fear, I can feel Your presence, Your desire to protect and guide
me. Thank You, Lord, for always staying close. Amen.

And they shall no more be a prey to the heathen,
neither shall the beast of the land devour them;
but they shall dwell safely, and none
shall make them afraid.

EZEKIEL 34:28

But whoso hearkeneth unto me shall dwell safely,
and shall be quiet from fear of evil.

PROVERBS 1:33

I will both lay me down in peace, and sleep:
for thou, LORD, only makest me dwell in safety.

PSALM 4:8

REPENTANCE

REPENTANCE IS WHAT leads to true transformation in our lives. When we turn from our past and follow Jesus into the future, we make a complete 180-degree turn to a new life. As the apostle Paul wrote, "Old things are passed away; behold, all things are become new" (2 Corinthians 5:17).

Lord, You are always here—to listen, to forgive, and to heal.
Help me to be repentant, to be willing to be brought low.
Heal me, Lord. Amen.

The time is fulfilled, and the kingdom of God
is at hand: repent ye, and believe the gospel.
MARK 1:15

And they went out, and preached
that men should repent.
MARK 6:12

The LORD is nigh unto them that are of a broken heart;
and saveth such as be of a contrite spirit.
PSALM 34:18

He healeth the broken in heart,
and bindeth up their wounds.
PSALM 147:3

Repent ye therefore, and be converted, that your sins
may be blotted out, when the times of refreshing shall
come from the presence of the Lord.
ACTS 3:19

But if the wicked will turn from all his sins that he
hath committed, and keep all my statutes, and do that
which is lawful and right, he shall surely live,
he shall not die. All his transgressions that he hath
committed, they shall not be mentioned unto him:
in his righteousness that he hath done he shall live.
EZEKIEL 18:21–22

RIGHTEOUSNESS

GOD DESIRES HIS children to live righteously and uprightly, but He knows that we can't do that on our own. True righteousness begins when we seek His will and direction for our lives. . .then follow daily after Him.

You, Lord, provide me with a lifetime of insight for leading a life that glorifies You and makes me more like You. Help me live every moment by the light of Your Word and become righteous through knowledge of Your Son, Jesus Christ. Amen.

For the LORD God is a sun and shield: the Lord
will give grace and glory: no good thing will
he withhold from them that walk uprightly.
PSALM 84:11

The young lions do lack, and suffer hunger:
but they that seek the LORD shall not
want any good thing.
PSALM 34:10

The fear of the wicked, it shall come upon him:
but the desire of the righteous shall be granted.
PROVERBS 10:24

*O Father, You have draped me in the garments of salvation
and wrapped me snugly in the robe of righteousness.
I am beautifully adorned by You—for You. You have
given me all I need to live a joyful life, and
I rejoice in Your gifts of beauty. Amen.*

Evil pursueth sinners: but to the righteous
good shall be repayed.
PROVERBS 13:21

A good man obtaineth favour of the LORD:
but a man of wicked devices will he condemn.
PROVERBS 12:2

But seek ye first the kingdom of God,
and his righteousness; and all these things
shall be added unto you.
MATTHEW 6:33

He that trusteth in his riches shall fall;
but the righteous shall flourish as a branch.
PROVERBS 11:28

So that a man shall say, Verily there is
a reward for the righteous.
PSALM 58:11

*Heavenly Father, keep me from making careless
choices that can develop into frightful consequences.
Guide me to choices that lead away from
the darkness of sin and into the light of righteousness.
Amen.*

For thou, LORD, wilt bless the righteous;
with favour wilt thou compass him as with a shield.
PSALM 5:12

Salvation belongeth unto the LORD:
thy blessing is upon thy people.
PSALM 3:8

Whether Paul, or Apollos, or Cephas,
or the world, or life, or death, or things present,
or things to come; all are yours;
And ye are Christ's; and Christ is God's.
1 Corinthians 3:22–23

He that spared not his own Son,
but delivered him up for us all,
how shall he not with him also freely give us all things?
Romans 8:32

Say ye to the righteous, that it shall be well with him:
for they shall eat the fruit of their doings.
Isaiah 3:10

Surely goodness and mercy shall follow me
all the days of my life: and I will dwell in the
house of the Lord for ever.
Psalm 23:6

SALVATION

UNTIL WE RECOGNIZE our sin, we won't think we've done anything wrong. But when God's Spirit gets hold of our lives, we begin to understand our need for salvation—and the only One who can provide it.

The theme of God's salvation appears in the Old Testament, but it comes to fruition in the life, death, and resurrection of His Son, Jesus. Through Him, people are saved as they answer His call to redemption.

I'm so glad that someone told me the Good News that You came to save me. Open my lips, Jesus, and provide the words that will share Your truth with many. Amen.

Jesus answered and said unto him, Verily, verily,
I say unto thee, Except a man be born again,
he cannot see the kingdom of God. Nicodemus saith
unto him, How can a man be born when he is old?
can he enter the second time into his mother's
womb, and be born? Jesus answered, Verily, verily,
I say unto thee, Except a man be born of water and of
the Spirit, he cannot enter into the kingdom of God.
That which is born of the flesh is flesh; and that
which is born of the Spirit is spirit. Marvel not
that I said unto thee, Ye must be born again.

JOHN 3:3–7

Therefore if any man be in Christ, he is a new creature:
old things are passed away; behold,
all things are become new.

2 CORINTHIANS 5:17

For he hath made him to be sin for us,
who knew no sin; that we might be made
the righteousness of God in him.

2 CORINTHIANS 5:21

And you hath he quickened,
who were dead in trespasses and sins.

EPHESIANS 2:1

For this is good and acceptable in the sight of God our Saviour; Who will have all men to be saved, and to come unto the knowledge of the truth.
1 TIMOTHY 2:3-4

Thank You, Father God, not only for saving me through Your Son, Jesus, but also for giving me Your power to make each day count for You. Help me not to leave Your Spirit on the shelf but to make Him part of my life always. Amen.

My little children, these things write I unto you, that ye sin not. And if any man sin, we have an advocate with the Father, Jesus Christ the righteous: And he is the propitiation for our sins: and not for ours only, but also for the sins of the whole world.
1 JOHN 2:1-2

And you, being dead in your sins and the uncircumcision of your flesh, hath he quickened together with him, having forgiven you all trespasses.
COLOSSIANS 2:13

This is a faithful saying and worthy of all acceptation. For therefore we both labour and suffer reproach, because we trust in the living God, who is the Saviour of all men, specially of those that believe.
1 TIMOTHY 4:9-10

But not as the offence, so also is the free gift. For if through the offence of one many be dead, much more the grace of God, and the gift by grace, which is by one man, Jesus Christ, hath abounded unto many.

ROMANS 5:15

But after that the kindness and love of God our Saviour toward man appeared, Not by works of righteousness which we have done, but according to his mercy he saved us, by the washing of regeneration, and renewing of the Holy Ghost; Which he shed on us abundantly through Jesus Christ our Saviour.

TITUS 3:4–6

You have not only promised today's salvation, Lord, but an eternity of life with You. When doubts assail, increase my hope. Help me to wait patiently for that final salvation. My hope lies in You alone. Amen.

But as many as received him, to them gave he power to become the sons of God, even to them that believe on his name: Which were born, not of blood, nor of the will of the flesh, nor of the will of man, but of God.

JOHN 1:12–13

SEEKING GOD

Do you ever feel like God is difficult to find? God never hides from us, but oftentimes the distractions and "stuff" of life—of our sinful nature—get between us and God, making Him hard to see. So instead of playing hide and seek, do some spring cleaning: You'll find Him standing near, with arms open wide.

Father, sometimes You seem to be far from me.
I look and see a great abyss between us, but as I pray,
my vision clears and I perceive a bridge that was there
all along. Thank You for building the bridge that
connects me to the peace You provide. Amen.

The LORD is with you, while ye be with him;
and if ye seek him, he will be found of you;
but if ye forsake him, he will forsake you.
2 CHRONICLES 15:2

Sow to yourselves in righteousness, reap in mercy;
break up your fallow ground: for it is time to seek the
LORD, till he come and rain righteousness upon you.
HOSEA 10:12

*Forgive me, Lord, for those times when I've doubted Your
presence. Let me close my eyes, hold out my hand, and know
that You are there. Thank You for being with me, Father.
Amen.*

But without faith it is impossible to please him: for he
that cometh to God must believe that he is, and that
he is a rewarder of them that diligently seek him.
HEBREWS 11:6

That they should seek the Lord, if haply they might
feel after him, and find him, though he be
not far from every one of us.
ACTS 17:27

The LORD is good unto them that wait for him,
to the soul that seeketh him.
LAMENTATIONS 3:25

But if from thence thou shalt seek the LORD thy God,
thou shalt find him, if thou seek him with
all thy heart and with all thy soul.
DEUTERONOMY 4:29

The hand of our God is upon all them for good
that seek him; but his power and his wrath
is against all them that forsake him.
EZRA 8:22

For thus saith the LORD unto the house of Israel,
Seek ye me, and ye shall live.
AMOS 5:4

And thou, Solomon my son, know thou the God of
thy father, and serve him with a perfect heart and
with a willing mind: for the LORD searcheth all hearts,
and understandeth all the imaginations of the
thoughts: if thou seek him, he will be found of thee;
but if thou forsake him, he will cast thee off for ever.
1 CHRONICLES 28:9

And they that know thy name will put their
trust in thee: for thou, LORD, hast not
forsaken them that seek thee.
PSALM 9:10

*What I seek is Your presence, Father. I trust You,
and You have promised to be with me forever, surrounding
me with Your sheltering arms. Thank You for
the security You bring to my life. Amen.*

And ye shall seek me, and find me, when ye shall
search for me with all your heart. And I will be found
of you, saith the LORD: and I will turn away your
captivity, and I will gather you from all the nations,
and from all the places whither I have driven you, saith
the LORD; and I will bring you again into the place
whence I caused you to be carried away captive.

JEREMIAH 29:13–14

SELF-RIGHTEOUSNESS

THE FACT IS, we *all* have sinned. A person who has failed only once is just as separated from God as the person who's sinned a million times. So to consider ourselves better than others—to be self-righteous—is silly. We're all equally guilty before God, and equally able to accept His salvation.

No matter how I strive to live in righteousness,
Lord, I will always fall short of Your standards.
Thank You for making my perfection possible in
the life to come. By myself, I would certainly fail.
With You, anything is possible. Amen.

There is a generation that are pure in their own eyes,
and yet is not washed from their filthiness.
There is a generation, O how lofty are their eyes!
and their eyelids are lifted up.

PROVERBS 30:12–13

The way of a fool is right in his own eyes:
but he that hearkeneth unto counsel is wise.

PROVERBS 12:15

Woe unto them that are wise in their own eyes,
and prudent in their own sight!

ISAIAH 5:21

*Father, I pray that I may be willing to ask for Your
guidance and follow it. Protect me from arrogance.
Direct me to Your truth. Amen.*

Yet thou sayest, Because I am innocent, surely his anger
shall turn from me. Behold, I will plead with thee,
because thou sayest, I have not sinned.

JEREMIAH 2:35

Seest thou a man wise in his own conceit?
there is more hope of a fool than of him.

PROVERBS 26:12

But he that glorieth, let him glory in the Lord.
For not he that commendeth himself is approved,
but whom the Lord commendeth.
2 Corinthians 10:17–18

He that is of a proud heart stirreth up strife:
but he that putteth his trust in the Lord shall be
made fat. He that trusteth in his own heart is a fool:
but whoso walketh wisely, he shall be delivered.
Proverbs 28:25–26

Father, I see Your ceaseless action in my life.
Day by day, You remove my rough edges.
You have made me into something better. Amen.

For if a man think himself to be something,
when he is nothing, he deceiveth himself.
Galatians 6:3

Let another man praise thee, and not thine own
mouth; a stranger, and not thine own lips.
Proverbs 27:2

Jesus said unto them, If ye were blind,
ye should have no sin: but now ye say,
We see; therefore your sin remaineth.
John 9:41

But we are all as an unclean thing,
and all our righteousnesses are as filthy rags;
and we all do fade as a leaf; and our iniquities,
like the wind, have taken us away.
ISAIAH 64:6

And he said unto them, Ye are they which justify
yourselves before men; but God knoweth your hearts:
for that which is highly esteemed among men is
abomination in the sight of God.
LUKE 16:15

Sexual Sins

A SHORT VERSION of the Bible's commands on this subject would be, "Don't!" The marital relationship is a picture of Christ and the Church, and God takes sexual conduct outside of marriage very seriously.

Lord, thank You for Your gift of sexual pleasures, but teach us to use them wisely, according to Your wishes for us. Keep us faithful to our spouses and to Your laws of self-control. Amen.

Now the body is not for fornication, but for the Lord;
and the Lord for the body.
1 CORINTHIANS 6:13

Flee fornication. Every sin that a man doeth is without
the body; but he that committeth fornication sinneth
against his own body. What? know ye not that your
body is the temple of the Holy Ghost which is in you,
which ye have of God, and ye are not your own? For ye
are bought with a price: therefore glorify God in your
body, and in your spirit, which are God's.
1 CORINTHIANS 6:18–20

There hath no temptation taken you but such as is
common to man: but God is faithful, who will not
suffer you to be tempted above that ye are able;
but will with the temptation also make a way to escape,
that ye may be able to bear it.
1 CORINTHIANS 10:13

Now concerning the things whereof ye wrote unto me:
It is good for a man not to touch a woman.
1 CORINTHIANS 7:1

I say therefore to the unmarried and widows, it is good for
them if they abide even as I. But if they cannot contain,
let them marry: for it is better to marry than to burn.
1 CORINTHIANS 7:8–9

Nevertheless he that standeth stedfast in his heart,
having no necessity, but hath power over his own will,
and hath so decreed in his heart that
he will keep his virgin, doeth well.

1 CORINTHIANS 7:37

Marriage is honourable in all, and the bed undefiled:
but whoremongers and adulterers God will judge.

HEBREWS 13:4

*Lord, I cannot help but be aware that it is difficult
to recover a good reputation once it has been tarnished.
Please help me keep Your presence in my life, and deliver
me from the temptations that surround me. Amen.*

These are they which were not defiled with women;
for they are virgins. These are they which follow the
Lamb whithersoever he goeth. These were redeemed
from among men, being the firstfruits
unto God and to the Lamb.

REVELATION 14:4

For this is the will of God, even your sanctification,
that ye should abstain from fornication.

1 THESSALONIANS 4:3

Know ye not that your bodies are the members
of Christ? shall I then take the members of Christ,
and make them the members of an harlot? God forbid.
1 CORINTHIANS 6:15

Who can find a virtuous woman?
for her price is far above rubies.
PROVERBS 31:10

*Father God, I know that emotions and feelings cannot be
trusted to lead me in the right direction. Thank You for
providing a clear set of directions for my life in Your Word.
Amen.*

The Lord knoweth how to deliver the godly out of
temptations, and to reserve the unjust unto
the day of judgment to be punished.
2 PETER 2:9

Blessed is the man that endureth temptation: for when
he is tried, he shall receive the crown of life, which the
Lord hath promised to them that love him.
JAMES 1:12

For in that he himself hath suffered being tempted,
he is able to succour them that are tempted.
HEBREWS 2:18

SHAME

WE ALL MAKE mistakes and do things we're not proud of. In fact, shame often arises from things we've done, words we've said, and thoughts we think. But when we repent of our sins—when we're covered in the forgiveness of Christ—we are blameless. Embrace the freedom that He offers, and live without shame!

Lord, You stand before the throne of Your Father and claim me as Your own, exempt from sin, judgment, and shame. Because of Your sacrifice, I am made worthy. Thank You. Amen.

For the scripture saith, Whosoever believeth
on him shall not be ashamed.
ROMANS 10:11

Then shall I not be ashamed, when I have
respect unto all thy commandments.
PSALM 119:6

And hope maketh not ashamed; because the love
of God is shed abroad in our hearts by the
Holy Ghost which is given unto us.
ROMANS 5:5

*Lord, thank You for granting me a new start every day,
free from the shame of the past, and proclaiming
that I am worth saving. Amen.*

For the which cause I also suffer these things:
nevertheless I am not ashamed: for I know
whom I have believed, and am persuaded
that he is able to keep that which I have
committed unto him against that day.
2 TIMOTHY 1:12

As it is written, Behold, I lay in Sion a stumblingstone
and rock of offence: and whosoever believeth
on him shall not be ashamed.
ROMANS 9:33

Study to shew thyself approved unto God,
a workman that needeth not to be ashamed,
rightly dividing the word of truth.
2 Timothy 2:15

Let my heart be sound in thy statutes;
that I be not ashamed.
Psalm 119:80

Yet if any man suffer as a Christian,
let him not be ashamed;
but let him glorify God on this behalf.
1 Peter 4:16

SICKNESS

SINCE THE FALL of man, our earthly bodies have had a shelf life. Whether it's sixty years or 105, our lifetimes include periods of sickness and ill health. And though these are difficult and stressful times, God is faithful to deliver His children from suffering.

Father God, whether it's physical sickness or spiritual, I believe You have provided healing through the sacrifice of Your Son, Jesus Christ. Keep me mindful of the price He paid so that I can enjoy a healthy relationship with You. Amen.

Is any sick among you? let him call for
the elders of the church; and let them pray over him,
anointing him with oil in the name of the Lord:
And the prayer of faith shall save the sick, and the
Lord shall raise him up; and if he have committed sins,
they shall be forgiven him. Confess your faults
one to another, and pray one for another,
that ye may be healed. The effectual fervent
prayer of a righteous man availeth much.

JAMES 5:14–16

And when he was come into the house, the blind men
came to him: and Jesus saith unto them, Believe ye that
I am able to do this? They said unto him, Yea, Lord.
Then touched he their eyes, saying, According to your
faith be it unto you. And their eyes were opened.

MATTHEW 9:28–30

Heal me, O LORD, and I shall be healed; save me,
and I shall be saved: for thou art my praise.

JEREMIAH 17:14

But that ye may know that the Son of man hath power
on earth to forgive sins, (then saith he to the sick of
the palsy,) Arise, take up thy bed, and go unto thine
house. And he arose, and departed to his house.

MATTHEW 9:6–7

And Jesus went about all Galilee, teaching in their synagogues, and preaching the gospel of the kingdom, and healing all manner of sickness and all manner of disease among the people. And his fame went throughout all Syria: and they brought unto him all sick people that were taken with divers diseases and torments, and those which were possessed with devils, and those which were lunatick, and those that had the palsy; and he healed them.

MATTHEW 4:23-24

Father, I pray for the sick among us, those whom medicine has failed, those whose only hope remains Your compassion and power. Stand by them in their time of suffering, wrap them in Your arms of love, and heal their bodies. Amen.

For I will restore health unto thee, and I will heal thee of thy wounds, saith the LORD.

JEREMIAH 30:17

And ye shall serve the LORD your God, and he shall bless thy bread, and thy water; and I will take sickness away from the midst of thee.

EXODUS 23:25

Who his own self bare our sins in his own body
on the tree, that we, being dead to sins, should live
unto righteousness: by whose stripes ye were healed.
1 PETER 2:24

But he was wounded for our transgressions,
he was bruised for our iniquities:
the chastisement of our peace was upon him;
and with his stripes we are healed.
ISAIAH 53:5

SIN, FREEDOM FROM

HABITUAL SIN FORCES us into cycles of bondage and guilt. First we sin—then we feel badly. When we realize it's a sin habit, how can we stop? We try but fail again, and the guilt grows. Jesus, though, paid the price for that sin—and through His grace we can know that if we ask, He is faithful to deliver us from the grip sin has on our lives.

What freedom from sin You have already given me—
but how much more sin needs to be removed from my life!
I trust in Your promise and look for the day when You return.
I long to be with You. Amen.

Then will I sprinkle clean water upon you,
and ye shall be clean: from all your filthiness,
and from all your idols, will I cleanse you. A new heart
also will I give you, and a new spirit will I put within
you: and I will take away the stony heart out of your
flesh, and I will give you an heart of flesh.

EZEKIEL 36:25–26

To him give all the prophets witness,
that through his name whosoever believeth
in him shall receive remission of sins.

ACTS 10:43

Knowing this, that our old man is crucified with him,
that the body of sin might be destroyed,
that henceforth we should not serve sin.
For he that is dead is freed from sin.

ROMANS 6:6–7

Therefore if any man be in Christ, he is a new creature:
old things are passed away; behold,
all things are become new.

2 CORINTHIANS 5:17

What shall we say then? Shall we continue in sin,
that grace may abound? God forbid. How shall we,
that are dead to sin, live any longer therein?

ROMANS 6:1–2

For sin shall not have dominion over you:
for ye are not under the law, but under grace.
ROMANS 6:14

*How can I repay Your gift of freedom from sin, Lord? I can't,
so take my life; keep me strong in You. My life is Yours,
Father. May I honor You all my days. Amen.*

Likewise reckon ye also yourselves to be dead indeed
unto sin, but alive unto God through
Jesus Christ our Lord.
ROMANS 6:11

SUCCESS

THE BIBLE OFTEN uses forms of the word *prosper* in describing success. "Prosperity" in scripture can describe not just earthly success, but an effective spiritual life, too. Many times over, God promises to prosper His people if they obey His will.

Dear Lord, I know You are able and willing to cleanse my life that has been tarnished by worldly ambitions. Thank You for creating in me a pure heart, focused on the eternal victory through Your Son. Amen.

And the Lord thy God will make thee plenteous in
every work of thine hand, in the fruit of thy body, and
in the fruit of thy cattle, and in the fruit of thy land,
for good: for the Lord will again rejoice over thee
for good, as he rejoiced over thy fathers.
Deuteronomy 30:9

And also that every man should eat and drink, and
enjoy the good of all his labour, it is the gift of God.
Ecclesiastes 3:13

And the Lord shall make thee plenteous in goods,
in the fruit of thy body, and in the fruit of thy cattle,
and in the fruit of thy ground, in the land
which the Lord sware unto thy fathers to give thee.
The Lord shall open unto thee his good treasure, the
heaven to give the rain unto thy land in his season,
and to bless all the work of thine hand: and thou shalt
lend unto many nations, and thou shalt not borrow.
And the Lord shall make thee the head, and not
the tail; and thou shalt be above only, and thou
shalt not beneath; if that thou hearken unto the
commandments of the Lord thy God, which I
command thee this day, to observe and to do them.
Deuteronomy 28:11–13

In the house of the righteous is much treasure:
but in the revenues of the wicked is trouble.
PROVERBS 15:6

Every man also to whom God hath given riches
and wealth, and hath given him power to eat thereof,
and to take his portion, and to rejoice
in his labour; this is the gift of God.
ECCLESIASTES 5:19

Lord, let me never become so determined to reach
my goals that I fail to see Your hand guiding me in the plan
that You have set for me. Temper my expectations
with thought and prayer. Amen.

Then shall he give the rain of thy seed, that thou shalt
sow the ground withal; and bread of the increase of
the earth, and it shall be fat and plenteous: in that day
shall thy cattle feed in large pastures.
ISAIAH 30:23

And he shall be like a tree planted by the rivers
of water, that bringeth forth his fruit in his season;
his leaf also shall not wither; and whatsoever
he doeth shall prosper.
PSALM 1:3

Riches and honour are with me; yea, durable riches
and righteousness. My fruit is better than gold, yea,
than fine gold; and my revenue than choice silver.
PROVERBS 8:18–19

Wealth and riches shall be in his house:
and his righteousness endureth for ever.
PSALM 112:3

*Father, You sent Your Son as a humble man—a man without
power or riches as the world counts power and riches.
Help me see the wisdom of that, and remind me
to live my own life in the same way. Amen.*

And I will send grass in thy fields for thy cattle,
that thou mayest eat and be full.
DEUTERONOMY 11:15

According as his divine power hath given unto us
all things that pertain unto life and godliness,
through the knowledge of him that
hath called us to glory and virtue.
2 PETER 1:3

But grow in grace, and in the knowledge of
our Lord and Saviour Jesus Christ. To him
be glory both now and for ever. Amen.
2 PETER 3:18

TRUST

TRUST IS KEY to any relationship—between parent and child, between friends, certainly between a husband and wife. And trust is the cornerstone of our relationship with God as well. Over and over, the Bible tells us to "trust in the Lord." If we can't trust Him, who *can* we trust?

Though I may not know the outcome of everything in my life, dear Father, I am trusting in You, and I know You care for all my needs. How my heart rejoices that I can trust in You! Amen.

God is our refuge and strength, a very present help
in trouble. Therefore will not we fear, though
the earth be removed, and though the mountains
be carried into the midst of the sea.

PSALM 46:1-2

For the LORD God is a sun and shield: the LORD will
give grace and glory: no good thing will he withhold
from them that walk uprightly. O LORD of hosts,
blessed is the man that trusteth in thee.

PSALM 84:11-12

Trust in the LORD, and do good; so shalt thou dwell in
the land, and verily thou shalt be fed. Delight thyself
also in the LORD: and he shall give thee the desires
of thine heart. Commit thy way unto the LORD;
trust also in him; and he shall bring it to pass.

PSALM 37:3-5

Trust in the LORD with all thine heart; and lean
not unto thine own understanding. In all thy ways
acknowledge him, and he shall direct thy paths.

PROVERBS 3:5-6

Fear not, little flock; for it is your Father's good
pleasure to give you the kingdom.

LUKE 12:32

Casting all your care upon him;
for he careth for you.
1 PETER 5:7

They that trust in the LORD shall be as mount Zion,
which cannot be removed, but abideth for ever.
PSALM 125:1

*Even when I face dark situations, I trust that You still walk
by my side. Today, Lord, I need courage to step forward.
Lift my heart with trust in You. Amen.*

Therefore take no thought, saying, What shall we eat?
or, What shall we drink? or, Wherewithal shall
we be clothed? (For after all these things do the
Gentiles seek:) for your heavenly Father knoweth
that ye have need of all these things.
MATTHEW 6:31–32

Blessed is that man that maketh the LORD his trust.
PSALM 40:4

WISDOM

WISDOM COMES FROM God, not people. But those who walk closely with Him can be good advisors when we need help. No one should avoid getting good advice when it's needed—and going first to God, then to faithful believers, will lead us into wise decisions.

Heavenly Father, You are a God of wisdom who loves it when Your children follow Your footsteps. Show me how to walk in Your ways, how to relate to others wisely and well, how to apply what You teach me to my daily life. Amen.

If any of you lack wisdom, let him ask of God,
that giveth to all men liberally, and upbraideth not;
and it shall be given him.

JAMES 1:5

And he will teach us of his ways,
and we will walk in his paths.

ISAIAH 2:3

Thank You for sharing Your wisdom with me, Lord.
You often let me realize the wisdom in Your rules and plans.
I begin to see the design You have for ruling the world.
Rule my life, also. Your judgments are always wise. Amen.

I will instruct thee and teach thee in the way which
thou shalt go: I will guide thee with mine eye.

PSALM 32:8

For God giveth to a man that is good in his sight
wisdom, and knowledge, and joy.

ECCLESIASTES 2:26

I will bless the LORD, who hath given me counsel:
my reins also instruct me in the night seasons.

PSALM 16:7

Then shalt thou understand the fear of the LORD,
and find the knowledge of God. For the LORD giveth
wisdom: out of his mouth cometh knowledge and
understanding. He layeth up sound wisdom for
righteous: he is a buckler to them that walk uprightly.
PROVERBS 2:5–7

Evil men understand not judgment:
but they that seek the LORD understand all things.
PROVERBS 28:5

And we know that the Son of God is come, and hath
given us an understanding, that we may know him that
is true, and we are in him that is true, even in his Son
Jesus Christ. This is the true God, and eternal life.
1 JOHN 5:20

For God, who commanded the light to shine
out of darkness, hath shined in our hearts,
to give the light of the knowledge of the glory
of God in the face of Jesus Christ.
2 CORINTHIANS 4:6

Behold, thou desirest truth in the inward parts: and in
the hidden part thou shalt make me to know wisdom.
PSALM 51:6

WORD OF GOD

WITHOUT GOD'S WORD, how would we know about God? That's why it's important for us to know what scripture says. That Word helps us know Jesus, whom the Bible also calls the Word. Through the written Word and His Son, God has shown us the way to Himself.

Father, I pray that the living water of Your Word will flow into my life. I believe You will allow me to accomplish much for Your glory as I gain knowledge from studying the Bible. Amen.

For I am not ashamed of the gospel of Christ:
for it is the power of God unto salvation
to every one that believeth.
ROMANS 1:16

Blessed is he that readeth, and they that hear the words
of this prophecy, and keep those things which are
written therein: for the time is at hand.
REVELATION 1:3

We have also a more sure word of prophecy;
whereunto ye do well that ye take heed, as unto a light
that shineth in a dark place, until the day dawn,
and the day star arise in your hearts.
2 PETER 1:19

For the word of God is quick, and powerful,
and sharper than any twoedged sword, piercing
even to the dividing asunder of soul and spirit,
and of the joints and marrow, and is a discerner
of the thoughts and intents of the heart.
HEBREWS 4:12

Search the scriptures; for in them ye think ye have
eternal life: and they are they which testify of me.
JOHN 5:39

For the commandment is a lamp; and the law is light;
and reproofs of instruction are the way of life.

PROVERBS 6:23

The entrance of thy words giveth light;
it giveth understanding unto the simple.

PSALM 119:130

*Lord, as I read and study Your Word and hear sermons
preached about it, I still have questions and much to learn.
I ask that You give me clear understanding of what
You are saying to me through it. Amen.*

The holy scriptures, which are able to make thee wise
unto salvation through faith which is in Christ Jesus.
All scripture is given by inspiration of God, and
is profitable for doctrine, for reproof, for correction,
for instruction in righteousness.

2 TIMOTHY 3:15–16

So then faith cometh by hearing,
and hearing by the word of God.

ROMANS 10:17

As newborn babes, desire the sincere milk of the word,
that ye may grow thereby.

1 PETER 2:2

Therefore shall ye lay up these my words in your heart and in your soul, and bind them for a sign upon your hand, that they may be as frontlets between your eyes.

DEUTERONOMY 11:18

This book of the law shall not depart out of thy mouth; but thou shalt meditate therein day and night, that thou mayest observe to do according to all that is written therein: for then thou shalt make thy way prosperous, and then thou shalt have good success.

JOSHUA 1:8

Father, I know that unless I make the effort to drink in Your Word, I am lost. The Bible says You are the source of water that quenches spiritual thirst. Thank You for granting to me the water that brings life everlasting. Amen.

And now, brethren, I commend you to God, and to the word of his grace, which is able to build you up, and to give you an inheritance among all them which are sanctified.

ACTS 20:32

Thy word is a lamp unto my feet, and a light unto my path.

PSALM 119:105

Being born again, not of corruptible seed,
but of incorruptible, by the word of God,
which liveth and abideth for ever.
1 PETER 1:23

*Dear Lord, I am thankful that You were kind enough to
provide Your Word. I pray for the will to read Your Word,
a mind to understand its meaning, and the
determination to act upon what I learn. Amen.*

Wherefore lay apart all filthiness and superfluity
of naughtiness, and receive with meekness the
engrafted word, which is able to save your souls.
But be ye doers of the word, and not hearers only,
deceiving your own selves. For if any be a hearer of the
word, and not a doer, he is like unto a man beholding
his natural face in a glass: For he beholdeth himself,
and goeth his way, and straightway forgetteth what
manner of man he was. But whoso looketh into
the perfect law of liberty, and continueth therein,
he being not a forgetful hearer, but a doer of the work,
this man shall be blessed in his deed.
JAMES 1:21–25

WORK

GOD WANTS US to work hard at everything we set our hands to. After all, our work brings Him glory! Just be sure to balance your workload with the people in your life, and follow God's example by resting at least one day per week.

I thank You, Lord, for my work and the opportunities
it brings me. May others not so blessed find the jobs
for which they are searching. May we all work
in a manner that brings glory to You. Amen.

And God blessed the seventh day, and sanctified it:
because that in it he had rested from all his work
which God created and made.

GENESIS 2:3

The LORD shall open unto thee his good treasure,
the heaven to give the rain unto thy land in his season,
and to bless all the work of thine hand: and thou shalt
lend unto many nations, and thou shalt not borrow.

DEUTERONOMY 28:12

Be ye strong therefore, and let not your hands be weak:
for your work shall be rewarded.

2 CHRONICLES 15:7

And in every work that he began in the service
of the house of God, and in the law, and
in the commandments, to seek his God,
he did it with all his heart, and prospered.

2 CHRONICLES 31:21

Even a child is known by his doings,
whether his work be pure, and whether it be right.

PROVERBS 20:11

Jesus saith unto them, My meat is to do the will
of him that sent me, and to finish his work.

JOHN 4:34

Then said they unto him, What shall we do,
that we might work the works of God? Jesus answered
and said unto them, This is the work of God,
that ye believe on him whom he hath sent.

JOHN 6:28–29

I have glorified thee on the earth: I have finished the
work which thou gavest me to do. And now, O Father,
glorify thou me with thine own self with the glory
which I had with thee before the world was.

JOHN 17:4–5

*Father, nudge me when I grow bored and sloppy at work.
I don't want to be the kind of worker who cuts corners and
gives less and less. I want to be known as a diligent worker.
Thank You for keeping me on track. Amen.*

Therefore, my beloved brethren, be ye stedfast,
unmoveable, always abounding in the work
of the Lord, forasmuch as ye know that
your labour is not in vain in the Lord.

1 CORINTHIANS 15:58

That ye might walk worthy of the Lord unto all
pleasing, being fruitful in every good work,
and increasing in the knowledge of God.
COLOSSIANS 1:10

Father, give me the sense to see through pretense and
recognize the truly competent workers around me,
whatever their position on the corporate ladder.
Let me choose my friends wisely so I may flourish
and contribute to the good of all. Amen.

For we hear that there are some which walk among
you disorderly, working not at all, but are busybodies.
Now them that are such we command and exhort by
our Lord Jesus Christ, that with quietness
they work, and eat their own bread.
2 THESSALONIANS 3:11-12

For God is not unrighteous to forget your work
and labour of love, which ye have shewed toward
his name, in that ye have ministered to the saints,
and do minister. And we desire that every one
of you do shew the same diligence to the full
assurance of hope unto the end.
HEBREWS 6:10-11

Except the LORD build the house, they labour in vain
that build it: except the LORD keep the city,
the watchman waketh but in vain.
PSALM 127:1

Let him that stole steal no more: but rather let him
labour, working with his hands the thing which is
good, that he may have to give to him that needeth.
EPHESIANS 4:28

Come unto me, all ye that labour and are heavy laden,
and I will give you rest.
MATTHEW 11:28

WORRY

GOD KNOWS THAT worry can easily overwhelm us. That's why He encourages us to trust in Him. We don't need to worry! When our concerns are in God's hands, they are in the right place.

Lord, help me forget the cares of the world for today;
fill my heart with light as Your blessings fall upon me
and I grow closer to You. Amen.

Be careful for nothing; but in every thing by prayer and
supplication with thanksgiving let your requests
be made known unto God. And the peace of God,
which passeth all understanding, shall keep
your hearts and minds through Christ Jesus.

PHILIPPIANS 4:6–7

God is our refuge and strength, a very present help in
trouble. Therefore will not we fear, though the earth
be removed, and though the mountains be carried
into the midst of the sea; Though the waters
thereof roar and be troubled, though the
mountains shake with the swelling thereof.

PSALM 46:1–3

For he shall be as a tree planted by the waters, and that
spreadeth out her roots by the river, and shall not see
when heat cometh, but her leaf shall be green; and
shall not be careful in the year of drought,
neither shall cease from yielding fruit.

JEREMIAH 17:8

And Jesus answered and said unto her, Martha,
Martha, thou art careful and troubled about many
things: But one thing is needful: and Mary hath
chosen that good part, which shall not
be taken away from her.

LUKE 10:41–42

But my God shall supply all your need according
to his riches in glory by Christ Jesus.
PHILIPPIANS 4:19

The LORD also will be a refuge for the oppressed,
a refuge in times of trouble. And they that know thy
name will put their trust in thee: for thou, LORD,
hast not forsaken them that seek thee.
PSALM 9:9–10

*The world presses in on me and defeats me,
despite my best efforts, until finally I call on You for help
and find You there, just waiting for me to ask.
Thank You, Lord, for helping me. Amen.*

Thou art my hiding place; thou shalt preserve me
from trouble; thou shalt compass me
about with songs of deliverance.
PSALM 32:7

He shall call upon me, and I will answer him:
I will be with him in trouble; I will deliver him,
and honour him.
PSALM 91:15

We are troubled on every side, yet not distressed;
we are perplexed, but not in despair; Persecuted,
but not forsaken; cast down, but not destroyed.
2 CORINTHIANS 4:8–9

And we know that all things work together
for good to them that love God, to them who
are the called according to his purpose.
ROMANS 8:28

*Forgive me my worldly attachments and anxieties, Lord.
Help me seek Your kingdom so I may live as a good example
of Your never-failing care and concern. Amen.*

And the work of righteousness shall be peace;
and the effect of righteousness
quietness and assurance for ever.
ISAIAH 32:17

WORSHIP

WE OFTEN THINK of worship as something we do at church on Sunday morning. But worship is actually a way of life—an everyday, every moment way to live in celebration of the One who is worthy of our praise.

Father, praising You must be high on my priority list.
Thank You that I am able to rejoice in You! Amen.

All the earth shall worship thee, and shall sing
unto thee; they shall sing to thy name.
PSALM 66:4

O come, let us worship and bow down:
let us kneel before the LORD our maker.
For he is our God; and we are the people
of his pasture, and the sheep of his hand.
PSALM 95:6-7

Exalt the LORD our God, and worship at his holy hill;
for the LORD our God is holy.
PSALM 99:9

Lord, sometimes I become spiritually dry.
Please send heavenly water to refresh my soul
and rejuvenate my worship. Amen.

Now when Jesus was born in Bethlehem of Judaea
in the days of Herod the king, behold, there came
wise men from the east to Jerusalem, Saying,
Where is he that is born King of the Jews? for we have
seen his star in the east, and are come to worship him.
MATTHEW 2:1-2

God is a Spirit: and they that worship him
must worship him in spirit and in truth.
JOHN 4:24